Indeed, Has

Paul

Really Said?

Indeed, Has Paul Really Said?

A Critique of N. T. Wright's Teaching on Justification

Published by:

The Armoury Ministries
www.thearmouryministries.com

*Unless otherwise indicated,
all Scripture references are taken from the New American Standard Bible®, Copyright ©
1960, 1962, 1963, 1968, 1971, 1972, 1973,
1975, 1977, 1995 by The Lockman Foundation
Used by permission. (www.lockman.org)*

Scripture quotations marked "NKJV" are taken from the New King James Version. Copyright © 1982 by Thomas Nelson, Inc. Used by permission. All rights reserved.

Indeed, Has Paul Really Said? *A Critique of N.T. Wright's Teaching on Justification*
ISBN: 978-1-935358-02-2
Copyright © 2008 by Michael J. Beasley.

Library of Congress Cataloging-in-Publication Data

Michael John Beasley

Indeed, Has Paul Really Said?
    Includes bibliographical references and index.
    Library of Congress Registration: TXu 1-590-612
    DREG: OCTOBER 1ST 2008

Cover image includes painting by Jacob Jordaens the elder (Flemish, 1593-1678), Adam and Eve (detail), 1645-1650, oil on canvas, 80 x 72 in. (203 x 182.9 cm). Toledo Museum of Art (Toledo, Ohio). Purchased with funds from Mrs. C. Lockhart McKlevy and from the Libbey Endowment, Gift of Edward Drummond Libbey, 1987-2011. Photo Credit: Photography Incorporated, Toledo.

Black and white drawing of tree and fruit by Hannah Rose Beasley, 2011, "God hath Said" (detail).

All rights reserved. No part of this book may be reproduced, stored in a retrieval system, or transmitted in any form or by any means – electronic, mechanical, photocopy, recording, or otherwise – without permission of the publisher, except for brief quotations in printed reviews. For more information go to: www.thearmouryministries.org.

Dedication

To Miss Betty

Whose godly example is a reminder that no matter what one's age, training, or experience may be, the child of God will always be a humble student of Scripture.

Isaiah 66:2

*"...to this one I will look,
to him who is humble and contrite of spirit,
and who trembles at
My word."*

Jeremiah 23:5-6 5

5 "Behold, the days are coming," declares the Lord, "When I shall raise up for David a righteous Branch; And He will reign as king and act wisely And do justice and righteousness in the land.

6 "In His days Judah will be saved, and Israel will dwell securely; And this is His name by which He will be called, 'The Lord our righteousness.'"

*Indeed, Has
Paul Really Said?*
~ *Table of Contents* ~

Introduction, A Catastrophic Conversation - 9

Chapter 1, The Righteousness of God, A Lexical Analysis - 19

Chapter 2, The Righteousness of God, The Forensic Context - 41

Chapter 3, The Righteousness of God, Paul's Apostleship - 65

Chapter 4, The Righteousness of God, The Whole Counsel of God - 87

Conclusion, A Tale of Two Contests - 109

Appendix - 115

Part I - 116

Part II - 122

Part III - 127

Part IV - 133

Part V - 139

Introduction

A
Catastrophic
Conversation

By way of introduction to our review of N.T. Wright's theology, it is important to note that not all theological conversations are spiritually profitable, especially when they result in either spiritual compromise or doctrinal ambiguity. Sadly, a significant number of theological conversations found within the contemporary church are rendering much in the way of such compromise and ambiguity, and the end result is that many are slipping deeper into the morass of error. Despite this, today's religious culture continues to herald the importance of such ecumenical conversations – conversations that enable markedly diverse groups to find common ground. Now I must be clear and say that unnecessary division in the body of Christ is sin, however what is rapidly being lost in the modern day is this crucial reality: any *unity* which forsakes truth *is an abomination*. Compromising dialogue may give the appearance of unity; however, to the Lord Himself such lukewarm pursuits deserve to be spewed out and rejected.[1] I offer this as a necessary prelude to our examination of Mr. Wright's work, *What Saint Paul Really Said;* because any analysis of another man's published views must be conducted by the standards of Scripture. In fact, since the Apostle Paul will be central to our study, we should remember that he himself understood the principles that govern our public and private defense of the faith - a principle that he fought to defend to the very end of his life.[2] Paul comprehended, contrary to the

---

[1] Revelation 3:16.

[2] 1 Timothy 4:7.

popular opinions of our own day, *that some doctrinal discourses do more harm than good.* This is most evident when Paul wrote to the church at Corinth as he gently, but firmly, rebuked them for their complicity with the errorists in their midst:

2 Corinthians 11:1-4: 1 I wish that you would bear with me in a little foolishness; but indeed you are bearing with me. 2 For I am jealous for you with a godly jealousy; for I betrothed you to one husband, that to Christ I might present you as a pure virgin. 3 But I am afraid, lest as the serpent deceived Eve by his craftiness, your minds should be led astray from the simplicity and purity of devotion to Christ. 4 For if one comes and preaches another Jesus whom we have not preached, or you receive a different spirit which you have not received, or a different gospel which you have not accepted, you bear this beautifully.

Paul had a godly jealousy for the Corinthians because they were abandoning their simple devotion to the bridegroom of the church: Jesus Christ. And how was this happening? Paul supplies the details in our aforementioned text: *"if one comes and preaches another Jesus whom we have not preached, or you receive a different spirit which you have not received, or a different gospel which you have not accepted, you bear this beautifully."* What Paul is describing here is the very same formula of disaster that was first concocted in the garden when Eve had her conversation with the serpent in the garden. The Apostle's parallel between the Corinthian church and Adam's bride is designed to remind his readers that they were engaging in a dangerous dialogue, just as the woman did with the serpent in Genesis 3. Consider the detail of the Apostle's language: when Paul said that the Corinthians responded to error by bearing it beautifully, he was indicating that they were accepting as valid or true the precepts of the evil one *without a contest.* To be more specific, the word *bear* represents the Greek word *anexesthe* – i.e. *forbearance*.[3] Clearly, such a word as this can speak of ungodly compromise or godly endurance, depending on the context. In the case of the Corinthians, they were tolerating, forbearing, and patiently listening to those who should have been refuted. Just as the Serpent in the garden should have been rebuked for his error, so too should the leadership of Corinth have dealt with the errorists in their midst:

2 Corinthians 11:13-15: 13 For such men are false apostles, deceitful workers, disguising themselves as apostles of Christ. 14 And no wonder, for even Satan disguises himself as an angel of light. 15 Therefore it is not surprising if his servants also disguise themselves as servants of righteousness; whose end shall be according to their deeds.

Paul's warnings concerning the dark influences of those men who stood against the Gospel of Christ are both chilling and stark. By these ancient standards, we too are warned in the modern day. For the church to engage in friendly conversations with errorists is plainly dangerous; and those who observe the complicity of leaders who do so will be inclined to entertain dangerous doctrines themselves. But in all of this we should remember that there is a need to be balanced in our application of the Apostle's warnings. While the church must certainly guard against mindless dialogue, she must also be careful not to hide from the very real problems which exist within the world of popular theology. Like Paul himself, we too should be willing to confront and expose those teachings which stand opposed to

---

[3] G. *anexesthe;* "...be patient with, put up with, endure..." Swanson, Dictionary of Biblical Languages: Hebrew Old Testament (Logos Research Systems), p. 462.

the core tenants of the Gospel. And when genuine Christians observe others drifting towards such catastrophic conversations, they should be filled with the same passionate jealously that filled the heart of Paul. For a Christian to feel any other way means that he is content to watch others be drawn into spiritual adultery. *May it never be.*

I fear that Eve's example of deception is not only fitting for that ancient church at Corinth, but that today, through theological movements like the *Emergent Conversation* along with the advocates of the *New Perspective on Paul*, contemporary Christianity has been drawn towards several forbidden fruits of false teaching. From the doctrine of hell, the law, Christ's resurrection, the atonement, and justification by faith, many today are *bearing well* teachings that have nothing to do with biblical exposition. It is within this broader scope of concern that I write this critique of N.T. Wright's book *What Saint Paul Really Said.* He and others in the modern day are generating a seismic shock wave within the contemporary church, and one can only wonder what effects this will have in the near future, as well as on subsequent generations. It is for this reason that I have decided to direct my attention towards one of the gravest errors being perpetuated today that has to do with the nature and work of *God's justification of the sinner*. Therefore, in order to make this my focus, I have chosen to critique the teachings of N.T. Wright on this matter, knowing that he is perhaps the most outspoken and the most read on this subject in recent years.

In introducing this material, it seems that N.T. Wright requires very little introduction at all. Most people reading this book will already be familiar with the teachings and background of Mr.

Wright. Wright holds doctorate degrees from Merton College, Oxford University, along with several other honorary doctorate degrees from other institutions. Since 2003 he has served as the Bishop of Durham for the Church of England and has become very popular here in America, mostly due to his published books and other literature. Perhaps he is best known for his part in advancing the theological movement known as *The New Perspective on Paul*, in keeping with men like E.P. Sanders and James Dunn. The most significant impact of *The New Perspective on Paul* has to do with its transformation of the doctrine of justification and imputation. Note that I do not say the *doctrines* of justification and imputation – but *doctrine* of justification and imputation. My use of the singular reference to *doctrine* is intentional as it recognizes the fact that God's work of *justifying* the sinner is indelibly linked to the concept of *imputation*. Therefore it is my conviction, and will be the argument of this book, that to separate these concepts is to gut justification of its crucial meaning. Prior to the publication of this book, I sent Mr. Wright a copy of my work in order to give him a chance to critique and evaluate my own analysis. His response to me is addressed in the appendix of this book.

All in all, I have to say that the popularity that surrounds Wright and his teachings has given me the sense of urgency to offer this public review. The impact that this man is having on the church cannot be ignored - it is already effecting how people think about the doctrine of justification and imputation.

A Catastrophic Conversation

The Spirit and Intent of This Work

To this date, I have never before written a book that focuses on an individual and his theology. Because of this, I feel a bit like a fish out of water. The tone of this work is something that I have been praying about and it is my desire to be appropriate regarding my topic and the polemic that is here employed. As to the matter of tone, let me refer you to another doctrinal controversy in history that involved Dr. Martin Luther and Desiderius Erasmus of Rotterdam. Their spat over the doctrine of the nature of man's will stands within history as perhaps one of the greatest theological contests ever conducted in the public eye. I offer you just one small sample that is representative of much of the rhetoric of that debate, where Martin Luther critiqued the teachings of Erasmus in the following manner:

> *"What shall I say here, Erasmus? You ooze Lucian from every pore; you swill Epicurus by the gallon. If you do not think this topic a necessary concern for Christians, kindly withdraw from the lists; we have no common ground; I think it vital...this is weak stuff, Erasmus; it is too much. It is hard to put it down to ignorance on your part, for you are no longer young, you have lived among Christians, and you have long studied the sacred writings; you leave me no room to make excuses for you or to think well of you."*[4]

By mentioning Luther's rebuke of Erasmus, it is my hope that you will view this critique of N.T. Wright in an appropriate light. In this day of hyper-genteelism, most people expect a milder form of banter which is less alarming to the senses. Many today have no desire to be startled by controversy, but I

---

[4] Martin Luther, The Bondage of the Will, trans. J.I. Packer and O.R. Johnston (Fleming H. Revell, A Division of Baker Book House Co, Grand Rapids, Michigan, 1997), p. 74.

would submit that much of the modern church is asleep and needs to be *alarmed* and *startled* concerning those who are creeping in unnoticed, *and in droves*. While in our weakness we might prefer a *quaint conversation* with others, we must remember that it is often necessary to engage in public *confrontations* for the sake of God's truth. All in all, it is not out of a love of controversy, but out of a love for Christ, for His glory, and for the eternal truth of His redemption that I do write.

As we focus on Wright's treatment of the doctrine of justification, my objective will be to keep matters as simple as possible. If you are not aware of Wright's beliefs regarding justification, then here is a sample of where Wright is coming from on this subject:

> *"Many Christians, both in the Reformation and in the counter-Reformation traditions, have done themselves and the church a great disservice by treating the doctrine of 'justification' as central to their debates, and by supposing that it described the system by which people attained salvation."* [5]

This quote is reflective of several statements made by Wright where he denies that justification is a concept which explains how a person is saved. In the following pages I will address N.T. Wright's approach to the term *"righteous,"* as well as the expression *"the righteousness of God,"* in four categories of thought -

---

[5] N.T. Wright, What Saint Paul Really Said, (William B. Eerdmans Publishing Company, Grand Rapids, Michigan, 1997), pp. 158-59.

A Catastrophic Conversation

1. A Lexical Analysis: *Wright's presentation of the expression "righteousness of God" as well as the term "justification" lacks a proper lexical analysis. Since this is the most elemental aspect of our study, we will begin by looking at the background and semantic domain of the term - righteousness.*

2. The Forensic Context: *The very concept of God's righteousness has an important, forensic (judicial) context. Therefore, in his book, Wright labors at length to establish a contextual framework for the concept of God's justification of the sinner, and this he does by presenting his own understanding of God's judiciary. It will be up to the reader to determine whether Mr. Wright has established a valid context for this discussion, or not.*

3. Paul's Apostleship: *Another core argument of Wright's has to do with the Apostle Paul's pedigree as a Pharisee. In this section the reader will be challenged to compare the Word of God with the testimony of Mr. Wright. Here, we will explore the question: "Was Paul's background as a Pharisee a significant factor concerning his theology as an Apostle of Jesus Christ?"*

4. The Whole Counsel of God: *In this section, we will consider the broader ramifications concerning N.T. Wright's argument as it relates to the rest of Holy Writ since the foundation of prophetic/apostolic revelation is a cohesive and unified one. By adjusting the meanings of one Apostle, Wright (whether intentionally or unintentionally) unveils much more than a new perspective on Paul.*

It is my prayer that the reader will not only become more informed regarding the teachings of N.T. Wright – but most importantly, that the glorious doctrine of justification and imputation would be heralded for the glory of our *Advocate with the Father* – Jesus Christ *the righteous*. Much is at stake here. Without a right understanding of justification, the church will fall prey to the serpent's deceptive whispers. May the Lord, by His precious grace, protect and preserve His people from such dainty morsels.[6]

---

[6] Proverbs 18:7-8.

Chapter 1

The Righteousness of God: A Lexical Analysis

This chapter will present a lexical analysis of the term *righteous*, because if we are to learn about the subject of *the righteousness of God*, as well as the concept of *justification*, then we must begin with a primitive analysis of the word's meaning. However, for the sake of contrast, we will first consider Wright's own lexical *conclusions* concerning the term *justification* and the expression *the righteousness of God*. By doing this, we can address the most important question that emerges from Wright's own writings: *Are his definitions of righteousness and justification valid?* Ultimately, every aspect of our study will converge on this crucial query because it is central to Wright's perspective on Paul. I will summarize his views as follows:

The Righteousness of God: Wright repeatedly insists that the central notion of *God's righteousness* is that of *His covenant faithfulness*. For example, he says: "...'the righteousness of God' would have one obvious meaning: God's own faithfulness to his promises, to the covenant."[7] Elsewhere, he summarizes his definition as follows: "When Paul uses the phrase 'the righteousness of God' he does not mean a quality or status which is attributed to human beings, but God's own faithfulness to the covenant and thereby to putting the whole world to rights (with human beings as the pilot project)."[8]

Justification: Consistent with his emphasis on God's covenant faithfulness, Wright emphasizes that justification points to the outworking of His covenant – not in terms of the salvation of sinners, but in terms of the eschatological confirmation of His people: "'justification' in the first century was not about how

---

[7] Wright, Saint Paul, p. 96.
[8] Wrightsaid Question and Answer Session, March 2004 (http://www.ntwrightpage.com/Wrightsaid_March2004.htm).

someone might establish a relationship with God. It was about God's eschatological definition, both future and present, of who was, in fact, a member of his people. In Sanders' terms, it was not so much about 'getting in', or indeed about 'staying in', as about 'how you could tell who was in'. In standard Christian theological language, it wasn't so much about soteriology as about ecclesiology; not so much about salvation as about the church."[9] Thus, he separates justification from the Gospel itself and concludes that "'the Gospel' creates the church; 'justification' defines it."

The distilled reality of what Mr. Wright is teaching is this: when Paul refers to *justification*, he is not referring to *the basis of our salvation as established by the righteous merit of Jesus Christ; instead, Paul is speaking of God's covenant faithfulness and eschatological victory as displayed among His people.* As he said, *it is not so much about soteriology as about ecclesiology.* Let me add one more observation before we examine Wright's definitions of justification and righteousness. Wright's climactic application of this new perspective on Paul renders a very broad-based ecumenism:

"Paul's doctrine of justification by faith impels the churches, in their current fragmented state, into the ecumenical task. It cannot be right that the very doctrine which declares that all who believe in Jesus belong at the same table (Galatians 2) should be used as a way of saying that some, who define the doctrine of justification differently, belong at a different table. The doctrine of justification, in other words, is not merely a doctrine which Catholic and Protestant might just be able to agree on, as a result of hard ecumenical endeavor. It is itself the ecumenical doctrine, the doctrine that rebukes all our petty and often culture-bound church groupings, and which declares that all who believe in Jesus belong

---

[9] Wright, Saint Paul, p. 119.

together in the one family...the doctrine of justification is in fact the great *ecumenical* doctrine."[10]

This point is crucial, especially if you missed the significance of his definitions of *the righteousness of God and justification.* Clearly, Wright's proposition is no small one. By transforming *justification* from a soteriological concept to that of an ecclesiastical one, Wright effectively eliminates the relevant distinctions between the doctrine of *infused righteousness* versus that of *imputed righteousness.* In Wright's understanding of what he has presented, a "...detailed agreement on justification itself, properly conceived, isn't the thing which should determine Eucharistic fellowship."[11] If what he is teaching is true, then the distinctions between Rome and Protestantism are "petty" ones. He promises that if Christians "could only get this right, they would find that not only would they be believing the gospel, they would be practicing it; and that is the best basis for proclaiming it."[12]

All of this is presented at the outset of our study so that the reader can better appreciate what is at stake. Wright is in no position, especially after these bold assertions, to say that his argument is somehow a non-essential one – *something with which the reader can disagree with no serious consequences.* According to Wright, if one's view of justification leads him away from a Catholic-Protestant ecumenism, then such a belief is petty and should be seen as that which belies the message and practice of *the true Gospel.* With such an assertion as this, let no

---

[10] Ibid., p. 158.
[11] Ibid., p. 159.
[12] Ibid.

A Lexical Analysis

one assume for a moment that this matter is *non-essential.* Let us be very clear here - Mr. Wright's lexical, historical, and grammatical analysis of *the righteousness of God,* and *justification,* has led him to some rather dangerous theological territory, and we would do well to proceed with caution. In this chapter, our study will be limited to the question regarding Wright's definition of *the righteousness of God* and *justification. Our primary investigation will therefore center on whether or not it is valid for Wright to isolate a word's meaning in such a monolithic way, understanding that most words have a semantic domain of denotative and connotative meaning and use.* Because of this, the student of Scripture will do well to allow the context of any Scripture to determine a particular word's use and meaning. Other considerations will be examined in the subsequent chapters to resolve whether or not there is any validity to his limited definitions of righteousness.

The central word of interest in our study is, in the Hebrew - *ṣedeq*, and in the Greek – *dikaios.* Of course, there are several variants of these words, but for now we will examine the root meaning of the term *righteous* from its Hebraic foundation. Lexically speaking, *ṣedeq* speaks of a *canonical standard or a measuring rule.*[13] Implicit within this thought is the idea of something that is straight[14] (i.e., a *reliable* measuring rod).

---

[13] Johannes P. Louw and Eugene Albert Nida, Greek-English Lexicon of the New Testament : Based on Semantic Domains, electronic ed. of the 2nd edition. (New York: United Bible societies, 1996, c1989), 1:743.

[14] *ṣādāq* - to be right, straight, i.q. *yāśār* as of a straight way (see *ṣedeq* Ps. 23:3)

Gesenius, W., & Tregelles, S. P. (2003). Gesenius' Hebrew and Chaldee lexicon to the Old Testament Scriptures. Translation of the author's Lexicon manuale Hebraicum et Chaldaicum in Veteris Testamenti libros, a Latin version of the work first published in 1810-1812 under title: Hebräisch-deutsches Handwörterbuch des Alten Testaments.; Includes index. (702). Bellingham, WA: Logos Research Systems, Inc.

Therefore, it is no surprise that the word is often used to speak of "the act of doing what is required according to *a standard*."[15] Even in the English language, the historic use of the word righteous[16] (Old English: *rihtwis*) is self descriptive in that the transitive-verbal use of *righteous* denoted the thought of "to set right; to justify; to do justice to; to make righteous."[17] As well, the ethical connotation of *rihtwis* described the man who walks in *right wisdom* according to God's standard, rather than the *crooked standard* of this world. In many respects, the semantic domain of our own English word is illustrative of the idea of *ṣedeq/dikaios* in its historic form and use. At the core of it all is the notion of God's infallible standard, whether by itself or as imitated by men. By contrast we should consider this: the mutable standards of men are no match for the unalterable standard of God Himself. As one whose background is in physics, I can't help but to think of the illustration found in the SI system of units.[18] From 1791 to 1983, the French Academy of Sciences attempted to achieve an unfailing standard of measurement found in what we call the meter. Their search for such a standard definition began with a fraction $(1/10,000,000^{th})$ of the Earth's meridian (from the equator to the North Pole), to the path-length of light as it travels in a vacuum in the time interval of $1/299,792,458^{second}$. The progression of these standards marks great improvements in defining the unit of

---

[15] Johannes P. Louw and Eugene Albert Nida, Greek-English Lexicon of the New Testament : Based on Semantic Domains, electronic ed. of the 2nd edition. (New York: United Bible societies, 1996, c1989), 1:743..

[16] The Oxford English Dictionary (unabridged) lists righteous as being used, historically, as an adjective, an adverb, a noun and as a verb. Though this last use is now obsolete, it is clear that it contained thought of distributive righteousness/justice. The Oxford English Dictionary 2nd Edition (Oxford University Press), Electronic Edition.

[17] Ibid.

[18] SI: F. Le Système international d'unités.

A Lexical Analysis

measurement known as the meter, and yet despite all these improvements over the years, there will always be an associated measure of error with this "standard." It is an amazing point to consider: with all of the refinements that can be introduced into the methods of establishing an absolute standard, there will always be an associated uncertainty simply because of the involvement of fallible men in what is a fallen and decaying world. I offer this to you as a contrasting illustration to the concept of God's righteousness. The *denotative* reality of *ṣedeq/dikaios* is that God's righteous standard is *immutable, holy, and perfect*. There is no associated uncertainty with His standard – because He is the *sine qua non* of all that might ever be called *righteous*. In view of this, the concept of mankind's ethical righteousness is always limited for the very simple reason that God's righteousness is infallible, perfect, and completely devoid of impurity.[19] When we consult lexical works on this subject, as in the case of The Theological Wordbook of the Old Testament, we find that the term *righteousness* reveals at least three *main* categories of thought within its semantic domain: 1. ethical, 2. forensic and 3. theocratic:

Ethical: This use of the word *ṣedeq* focuses on a horizontal application of thought as it relates to man's fallible pursuit of God's righteous standard found in His Word. Therefore "the man who is righteous tries to preserve the peace and prosperity of the community by fulfilling the commands of God in regards to others."

---

[19] Isaiah 64:6 For all of us have become like one who is unclean, And all our righteous deeds are like a filthy garment; And all of us wither like a leaf, And our iniquities, like the wind, take us away.

It is this aspect of righteousness in which we see man's "conformity to the standards set out in the word of God."[20]

Forensic: In many contexts we see the term righteousness being used in terms of the judiciary of God. "The forensic aspect of *ṣedeq* applies to the equality of all, rich and poor, before the law. The righteous one, the *ṣăḏiq*, is not to be put to death (Ex 23:7) for the law does not condemn him."[21] Noah, Daniel and Job are identified as righteous men (Ezek 14:14, 20), but antecedent to these declarations, we have the example of Abraham: "Gen 15:6 teaches that Abraham received Isaac as his heir because his trust in God's promises was accounted as righteousness."[22]

Theocratic: Here we have *ṣedeq* being used to speak of God's own kingdom rule. Of course, it is this category of thought which formulates the basis for the *ethical and forensic* uses of the word. God's own essential righteousness, His prerogative of eschatological judgment, and His covenant faithfulness as displayed in His deliverance of His people,[23] are all thoughts that are variously supplied in this use of *ṣedeq*.

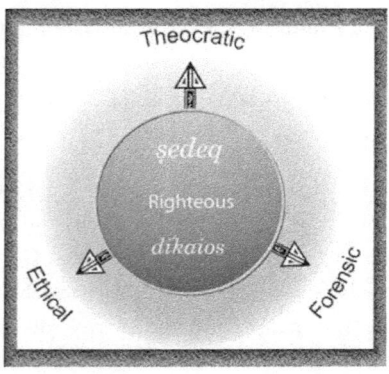

It must be noted that in every one of these categories of genuine righteousness there is an implicit notion of God's ontological nature of

---

[20] Harris, R. L., Harris, R. L., Archer, G. L., & Waltke, B. K. Theological Wordbook of the Old Testament (Electronic Edition Moody Press, Chicago, 1999, c1980) p. 753.
[21] Ibid.
[22] Ibid., p. 754.
[23] Ibid.

righteousness. After all, man's pursuit of genuine righteousness in this life constitutes a pursuit of God's righteousness as revealed in His Word; or when we speak of God's judiciary, we are speaking of the disclosure of God's own righteousness in His judgment or pardon of sinners; and when we speak of the establishment of God's kingdom, through the faithful redemption of His people, we are acknowledging His *rightness* (justice) in doing so. This brief review of the word *righteous* is designed to help the reader appreciate the concept of a semantic domain. In any semantic domain, there will usually be a spread of *connotative* meanings that extend beyond the root meaning. Ultimately, the student of Scripture must be careful to consider the word's own context if he is to comprehend the matter of meaning. Therefore, in any lexical examination it is one's responsibility to research the root idea of a word, and then to expand that research to the multiple contexts and time frames in which the word is used. It should therefore be no surprise that the Theological Wordbook of the Old Testament lists eight branches of use, concerning our word *ṣedeq*, and these are listed as related extensions of the aforementioned categories of *theocratic, forensic, and ethical.* Here is a summary:

1. Conformity to a standard (Gen. 15:6).

2. The character and nature of God (Deut. 32:4).

3. God's ultimate standard for human conduct (*ṣedāqā*).

4. God's judgment of moral transgression (Exod. 9:27).

5. God's vindication of the righteous (Gen. 18:25).

6. God's work of justification as "seen when David pleads for forgiveness (Ps. 51:14 [H 16])."[24]

7. "The word describes the righteous standing of God's heirs to salvation, with no charge to be laid against them (Isa 54:17), this righteousness, actually possessed by Messiah (Jer. 23:6), is bestowed by him, thus pointing toward the NT doctrine of Christ our righteousness. The righteousness of God's heirs of salvation is the righteousness of the Messiah attributed to them by God through faith in the redemptive work of Messiah in which God declares them righteous only because of the grace provided through that redemptive work."[25]

8. The benevolent acts of the godly (Ps. 112:9).

The purpose of this summary is to offer a broader context for our original query about Wright's limited definition of God's righteousness (covenant faithfulness). His limited meaning reduces the aforementioned analysis of *ṣedeq* and *dikaios* to an extremely narrow margin of connotation. Such a procedure places the interpreter in a very dangerous position by leaving him without the necessary lexical tools required to evaluate word meanings *in context*. Poorly constructed word studies can wreak havoc on an interpreter's conclusions when examining the text of Scripture. Consider this as an example:

Philippians 4:6 Be anxious [*merimnate*] for nothing, but in everything by prayer and supplication with thanksgiving let your requests be made known to God.

---

[24] Ibid., p. 754.
[25] Ibid.

A Lexical Analysis

At the root level *merimnaō* speaks of the idea of being concerned for someone or something. In the context of Philippians 4:6, this term is employed in order to speak of *sinful anxiety*. Now consider this: if we were to take Philippians 4:6 as our only clue concerning Paul's use and understanding of the Greek word *merimnaō*, then we might be tempted to conclude that this word's semantic domain is limited to *sinful anxiety* alone. However, Paul also used this same term in contexts which speak of godly concern. We see this in the case of Epaphroditus (Phil. 2:20), and in the case of Paul's instructions to the church at Corinth:

> 1 Corinthians 12:24-25: 24 ...But God has so composed the body, giving more abundant honor to that member which lacked, 25 that there should be no division in the body, but that the members should have the same *care* [*merimnōsin*] for one another.

The contexts of Philippians 4:6, 2:20, and 1 Corinthians 12:25 clearly reveal that Paul used this word anxiety/care in a multifaceted fashion. At the most primitive level *merimnaō* denotes care/concern. Contextually speaking, such care/concern can be either godly or ungodly; but can you imagine someone insisting that Paul only meant one thing every time that he used this word? Such an approach would be seen for what it really is – an undisciplined and dangerous procedure that has nothing to do with serious lexical analysis. As this is the case for

merimnaō, so it is the case for any other Scriptural word, to include the subject of our study here - *ṣedeq/dikaios*.

Based upon the normal principles of lexical analysis alone, it is a wonder that Wright insists on this limited interpretation of the term *righteousness*. One of his earliest justifications for this conclusion is found in the following paragraph:

> "For the reader of the Septuagint, the Greek version of the Jewish scriptures, 'the righteousness of God' would have one obvious meaning: God's own faithfulness to his promises, to the covenant."[26]

This confident assertion is offered by Wright with no significant qualifications or explanations. By this brief interjection of his, the reader is expected to accept the thought that the Septuagint (LXX) does what Wright himself does: reduce the concept of righteousness to a monolithic idea of God's covenant faithfulness. But Wright's mention of the LXX is rather telling. While there are occasions where the LXX translators favored a *connotative* emphasis on God's faithfulness,[27] it must be remembered that this does not dominate the translation. As well, as a translation of the Hebrew Scriptures, the Septuagint is not without its translational problems and nuances and therefore should be used very carefully as a witness to the O.T. Scriptures themselves.[28] Ultimately, Wright's sole deference to

---

[26] Wright, Saint Paul, p. 96.

[27] "In the LXX the use of *ṣĕdāqāh* for God's dispensing of salvation is carried to such a point that *dikaiosúnē* can even be used for *ḥesed* (Gn. 19:19; 20:13; 21:23; 24:27; 32:10; Ex. 15:13; 34:7; Prv. 20:22, Mas. 20:28) when *eleos* is the more usual rendering." Kittel, Gerhard, Geoffrey William Bromiley, and Gerhard Friedrich, Theological Dictionary of the New Testament.Vol. 2, ed. (Grand Rapids, MI, 1964-c1976), pp. 174-226.

[28] "Where there is a genuine deviation from the MT (Masoretic Text) on the part of other witnesses (and the deviation is not simply a matter of translator's interpretation) and both

A Lexical Analysis

the LXX proves nothing concerning the Apostle Paul's meaning and use of *ṣedeq/dikaios*. In fact, when we examine Paul's citations of the O.T., we find that his references to God's righteousness are consistent with those of the historic-Hebraic idea, contrary to Wright's supposition. The reader should remember that much of Wright's argument focuses on Paul's expression - *the righteousness of God*. Wright contends that this expression converges to the sole notion of God's covenant faithfulness,[29] and thus he declares in chapter six that this rules out the "logic chopping" idea of *imputed righteousness*,[30] and as well he says: "we may rule out the old idea of the *iustitia distributive*[31] as a Latin irrelevance." What Wright regards as a *quod erat demonstrandum (QED)*[32] is utterly unconvincing, and reveals a crucial omission on his part. What is missing in his argument is any textual evidence revealing that Paul was in fact influenced by a monolithic *ṣedeq/dikaios/covenant-faithfulness* form of thinking, as instigated by a presumed influence of the LXX.[33] Since it is Wright who argues thus, it

---

readings seem equally sensible, then the preference should normally be given to the MT." Gleason L. Archer, A Survey of Old Testament: Introduction (Moody Press, Chicago), p. 61.

[29] Wright, Saint Paul, p. 101.

[30] Ibid. p. 102.

[31] L. iustitia distributive ~ distributive justice.

[32] L. *Quod erat demonstrandum (QED)* ~ which was to be demonstrated (but does not require debate).

[33] The closest that Wright comes to offering a specific example of this is found on page 99 where he argues that Paul is quoting from Psalm 143 in Romans 3:20. In reality, Paul is not quoting from Psalm 143, and a strict comparison between Psalm 143:2 and Romans 3:20 reveals that there is only one word in common between the two texts. But this fact does not prevent Wright from extrapolating the following conclusion: "'Enter not into judgment with your servant, O Lord, for in your sight shall no man living be justified!' Psalm 143, in fact, from which those words come, forms a typical statement of the Jewish hope: covenantal, shot through with metaphorical law-court overtones. It also happens to be the psalm Paul quotes at a crucial turn in his argument (Romans 3:20)." Wright, Saint Paul, p. 99.

would be much more convincing if he could demonstrate such an influence in the LXX through specific O.T. passages used by Paul in connection with *the righteousness of God*. If Paul's expression, *the righteousness of God,* is the product of the Septuagint's direct influence (with a covenant-faithfulness coloration), then we should be able to detect it directly when he quotes the O.T. With this crucial idea in hand, the reader should first understand that the phrase *the righteousness of God* (*dikaiosúnē theou*) appears nowhere in the LXX, therefore Wright's effort to connect this expression to the LXX is by nature *implicit*, rather than *explicit*.[34] Additionally, when we explore Paul's O.T. support for his references to *the righteousness of God,* we discover something very interesting. Of the six occasions where Paul speaks of the *dikaiosúnē theou* we find that three of those occurrences are found in Romans chapter three, marking a maximal effort on his part to clarify what this expression actually means. And what O.T. text does Paul consult in order to initiate his look at *the righteousness of God*? It is Psalm 51:4, where David's sin is revealed as an example of how God is to be "found true, though every man be found a liar" (Romans 3:4a), and subsequently that "our unrighteousness demonstrates the righteousness of God" (Romans 3:5):

Psalm 51:1-4 1 For the choir director. A Psalm of David, when Nathan the prophet came to him, after he had gone in to Bathsheba. Be gracious to me, O God, according to Thy lovingkindness; According to the greatness of Thy compassion blot out my

---

[34] It should be remembered that it is Wright who argues that the N.T. writers maintained a slavish devotion to the LXX. Thus the point being raised here is designed to expose the fallacy of Wright's supposition, not to agree with it.

transgressions. 2 Wash me thoroughly from my iniquity, And cleanse me from my sin. 3 For I know my transgressions, And my sin is ever before me. 4 Against Thee, Thee only, I have sinned, And done what is evil in Thy sight, so that Thou art justified when Thou dost speak, and blameless when Thou dost judge.

Paul's quotation of Psalm 51:4 supplies the basis for what he says next:

Romans 3:5-6: 5 But if our unrighteousness demonstrates the righteousness of God, what shall we say? The God who inflicts wrath is not unrighteous, is He? (I am speaking in human terms.) 6 May it never be! For otherwise how will God judge the world?

The context of Paul's argument, as well as David's condemnation, is this: in view of mankind's sin, all are condemned by the *standard of the righteousness of God*. The picture that Paul supplies is that of the judiciary of God, where the Lord alone is justified when He declares our condemnation in view of our sin. When the Lord exposed David's sin by means of Nathan the prophet, David could do nothing else but confess his guilt in the presence of this righteous God. God is not condemned by men, rather all men stand under the righteous condemnation of God:

Romans 3:4 "...let God be found true, but every man a liar; as it is written, THAT THOU MIGHTEST BE JUSTIFIED IN THY WORDS, AND MIGHTEST PREVAIL WHEN THOU COMEST INTO JUDGMENT." [ASV]

Paul's use of David's confession is very important. David is not seeking covenant vindication against the Gentile nations, rather he is seeking God's mercy and forgiveness *in view of his own sin*. Thus, David is a crucial example for Paul's argument: in view of *all men's sin* (for there is no distinction whether Jew or Greek)[35] God is *justified when He speaks* and blameless *in judgment.* As the Judge of the world, how could we expect anything less (Romans 3:6)? Now, let's consider the details of Paul's citation of Psalm 51:4 as it relates to *God's righteousness* and *His judgment.* The corresponding Hebrew terms here are: *tiṣdāq* (justified, from *ṣedeq* - righteous) and *beśāpṭek* (judge, from *śāpāṭ* to judge or govern). These terms show us that Paul sought to reveal God's *judicial righteousness* in dealing with sin since it was David himself who understood that God's *righteous standard* would not bend, even for the monarch of Israel; though David was a descendent of Abraham, and though he was Israel's chosen king, there can be no distinction made among men in view of their sin, *for all have sinned and fall short of God's glory (Romans 3:23).*

We must also note that Paul's citation from the O.T. clearly reveals the proper concept of, and relationship between, *ṣedeq* and *dikaios.* This is made evident when we consult the LXX along with Paul's citation of Psalm 51:4. Clearly, this critical citation, along with the overall context of Psalm 51, is absent of the supposed LXX colorations of which Wright himself has strenuously emphasized.[36] When David cries out for God's lovingkindness in Psalm 51:1, he used the Hebrew word *ḥesed.*

---

[35] Romans 3:22-23.

[36] Consider, once again, this prior citation: "In the LXX the use of *ṣēdāqāh* for God's dispensing of salvation is carried to such a point that *dikaiosúnē* can even be used for *ḥesed* (Gn. 19:19; 20:13; 21:23; 24:27; 32:10; Ex. 15:13; 34:7; Prv. 20:22, Mas. 20:28) when *eleos* is the more usual rendering." Kittel, TDNT, pp. 174-226. While it is true that the LXX *translators* made such choices, what is at stake here is the question of the Apostle Paul's inspired use of the O.T. citations in question. Ultimately, Paul's employment of the O.T. is devoid of the very LXX colorations which Wright asserts.

A Lexical Analysis

Not surprisingly, we find that the LXX employs the more normative Greek word *éleos* (compassion, *faithfulness*, lovingkindness); and when David declares that God is "justified" in His declared judgment (Psalm 51:4/Romans 3:4), the LXX uses *dikaiōthēs* as expected (...*opōs án dikaiōthēs en toís lógois sou kai nikēsēs en tō krínesthai' se*). Thus Wright's argument for a *ṣedeq/dikaios/covenant-faithfulness* coloration in Paul's thinking does not survive the scrutiny of the biblical evidence. Yet, if we were to submit to Wright's insistence that *the righteousness of God* has "one obvious meaning: God's own *faithfulness* to his promises" then this would yield a rather serious miscarriage of meaning in Paul's argument. Paul's initial argument in Romans chapter three focuses on God's righteousness which clearly reveals mankind's sinful condemnation. It is this concept of God's judicial righteousness to which Paul points in order to reveal the broader argument concerning:

God's Judgment of Sinners (Romans 3:1-20): The Lord is righteous when condemning men.

God's Justification of Sinners (Romans 3:21-30): He is righteous in forgiving and redeeming those who believe in Christ through the merit of Christ's propitiation: "...that He might be just and the justifier of the one who has faith in Jesus" (Romans 3:26).

This twofold argument further advances his premise in the first chapter of Romans concerning the revelation of God's righteousness in terms of *justification (through faith in Christ) and judgment (in view of our sin):*

> **God's Justification of Sinners (Romans 1:16-18):** 16 For I am not ashamed of the gospel, for it is the power of God for salvation to everyone who believes, to the Jew first and also to the Greek. 17 For in it the righteousness of God is revealed from faith to faith; as it is written, "But the righteous man shall live by faith."
>
> **God's Just Judgment of Sinners (Romans 1:18):** 18 "For the wrath of God is revealed from heaven against all ungodliness and unrighteousness of men..."

I should remind the reader here that the revelation of God's righteousness also reveals His faithfulness. What I am presenting in this book in no way nullifies that precious and important fact. However, what cannot be assumed is that God's covenant faithfulness somehow serves as a monolithic substitute for the historic and multifaceted connotation of God's righteousness. In other words, though these concepts are wonderfully related, they are still distinct. Paul's repeated theme throughout Romans 1-3 is that *God's righteousness is faithfully revealed* through the distribution of His just judgment, and through the gift of justification to everyone who believes in Christ. This then leads him to showcase Abraham as the father of those who believe in the very next chapter. On three occasions in chapter 4 Paul quotes from Genesis 15:6 (Romans 4:3, 9 & 22) in order to remind his readers that "Abraham believed God, and it was credited to him as righteousness." By this repetition, he underscores his earlier point about the Gospel being the power of God unto salvation – not the works of the Law:

> Romans 4:10-13: 10 How then was it credited? While he was circumcised, or uncircumcised? Not while circumcised, but while

A Lexical Analysis

uncircumcised; 11 and he received the sign of circumcision, a seal of the righteousness of the faith which he had while uncircumcised, so that he might be the father of all who believe without being circumcised, that righteousness might be credited to them, 12 and the father of circumcision to those who not only are of the circumcision, but who also follow in the steps of the faith of our father Abraham which he had while uncircumcised. 13 For the promise to Abraham or to his descendants that he would be heir of the world was not through the Law, but through the righteousness of faith.

Of course, Paul is not saying that there are no antecedent examples of those who were redeemed by grace through faith. Clearly, Hebrews 11 speaks of Abel, Enoch, and Noah (among other men of old, v.2) who stand in biblical history as reminders that "without faith it is impossible to please God."[37] Paul is not nullifying these examples, but instead he highlights Abraham's example for at least two reasons: *First*, it is because of Abraham's centrality in God's Word as the one who received the grace of salvation before he was given the sign of circumcision; *Second*, Abraham's example is repeatedly heralded by Paul in order to give prominence to the Gospel-truth of *justification by faith alone - "Abraham believed God, and it was credited to him as righteousness."* The fact that God's gift of justification (Romans 3:24) comes by means of faith alone, not works, was central to Paul's defense of the Gospel. Thus, God's righteousness is credited/imputed by means of faith, and by this the believer in Christ is no longer condemned (Romans 3 & 5:1), but has a *present and indicative*[38] peace with

---

[37] Hebrews 11:6.

[38] The believer's hope is not a delayed one, that must wait for the final judgment of God, but is ongoing (present) and indicative (real) as indicated by Paul's use of the *present active indicative* verb: éxomen (eirḗnēn éxomen pros theon – we *have* peace with God).

God through the Lord Jesus Christ. Again, Paul's repeated expression concerning *the righteousness of God* is clarified through his teaching regarding *1. God's judgment of the impenitent, and 2. God's gift of justification to everyone who believes in Christ*. A more careful and contextual analysis of Romans 1-5 reveals this. But Mr. Wright's stilted use of Paul's expression *the righteousness of God* is shown for what it is, especially in Romans chapter 3 where Paul's citation of Psalm 51:4 utterly dismantles Wright's argument that *ṣedeq/dikaios* converges on the sole meaning of *covenant faithfulness* as that which is supposedly devoid of any notion of *God's punitive justice or imputed righteousness*. Instead, David's personal condemnation, contrition, and confession of faith (Psalm 51) supports Paul's emphasis concerning the need for condemned and sinful men to confess their sin to God and to trust in Christ alone. As men appear before the tribunal of God, this is their only hope:

> Romans 3:21-24: 21 But now apart from the Law the righteousness of God has been manifested, being witnessed by the Law and the Prophets, 22 even the righteousness of God through faith in Jesus Christ for all those who believe; for there is no distinction; 23 for all have sinned and fall short of the glory of God, 24 being justified as a gift by His grace through the redemption which is in Christ Jesus;

God's righteous judgment *is what we deserve;* but God's unmerited justification is a "*gift* by His grace." Thus, whether in judgment or in redemption, God is *righteous - let God be found true, though every man be found a liar*. In all of this, we can confess with Paul as he wrote later in Romans: "Behold then the kindness and severity of God" (Romans 11:22).

A Lexical Analysis

Wright's attempt to retool the definitions of *ṣedeq/dikaios* & *dikaiosunē* reveals a strange agenda, especially since his procedures lack the critical analysis necessary to understand the historical languages of the Bible. Sadly, Mr. Wright invests much paper and ink in order to insist that the expression - *the righteousness of God* should be seen as having "one obvious meaning" - God's covenant faithfulness. In order to get to this conclusion it was necessary that Wright reduce the semantic domain of *ṣedeq/dikaios* & *dikaiosunē* to a very limited train of thought. By this the necessary tools of lexical, historical, and contextual analysis are discarded and are replaced with a reckless and oversimplified use of the Septuagint. All of this raises a number of questions regarding his understanding of the authority of Scripture as well as the proper methodology of interpretation. Additionally, one must wonder if Wright expects the other writers of Holy Writ to be constrained to his understanding of *ṣedeq/dikaios* & *dikaiosunē* – or does this system of thought apply only to the Apostle Paul? If it only applies to the Apostle Paul, then what can be said of the unity of the N.T. writers concerning the subject of God's righteousness?

These are the questions that we must address in our continuing study, but for now we must take our analysis of *ṣedeq/dikaios* & *dikaiosunē* to the next level by considering the historical use of these terms in the context of God's judiciary. It is to this very inquiry that Wright takes his discussion, and so we must proceed by following him there.

Chapter 2

The Righteousness of God and The Forensic Context

Indeed, Has Paul Really Said?

At this point it is perhaps obvious to the reader that the task of critiquing Wright's view of justification is not an easy one. Wright's maladroit transformations of historic orthodoxy require some very "creative bits of exegesis *en route,*" to use his own words.[39] But by reducing his argument to our four simple points it is my hope that the reader will be able to comprehend Wright's key errors with ease. As mentioned in the introduction, our examination of Wright's presentation of *the righteousness of God* centers on four main points of analysis: *1. Lexical Analysis; 2. Forensic Context; 3. Paul's Apostleship, and 4. The Full Counsel of God.* We continue in this chapter by examining our second query regarding Wright's treatment of the word *justification in its forensic context.* It is to this point of study that Wright establishes a critical foundation concerning the concept of justification as it relates to the Jewish courtroom scene. Once he sets the stage with what he believes to be the Jewish courtroom of the O.T., he then posits the notion that God's forensic justification of the sinner can only refer to one's legal status apart from any notions of *imputation.* To the casual observer, this description of his may appear to be adequate, but it is not. Sadly, Wright offers no solid Scriptural support for what he presents, and the reader is expected to accept his partial portrait of the Hebrew law court as a key building block for his understanding of *ṣedeq/dikaios* & *dikaiosunē.* Thus, in his book, Wright offers the following as a description of the Judaic courtroom:

---

[39] Wright, Saint Paul, p. 190. Here I am borrowing from Wright's own critique of Gerd Theissen's work, *Psychological Aspects of Pauline Theology:* "A bit of a *tour de force,* and not always completely convincing. Fascinating attempt to understand Paul psychologically, with some creative bits of exegesis *en rout.*"

The Forensic Context

"Part of the particular flavour of the term (righteousness of God), however, comes from the metaphor which it contains. 'Righteousness' is a forensic term, that is, taken from the law court. This needs to be unpacked just a bit. In the (biblical) Jewish law court there are three parties: the judge, the plaintiff and the defendant. There is no 'director of public prosecutions'; all cases take the form of one party versus the other party, with the judge deciding the issue."[40]

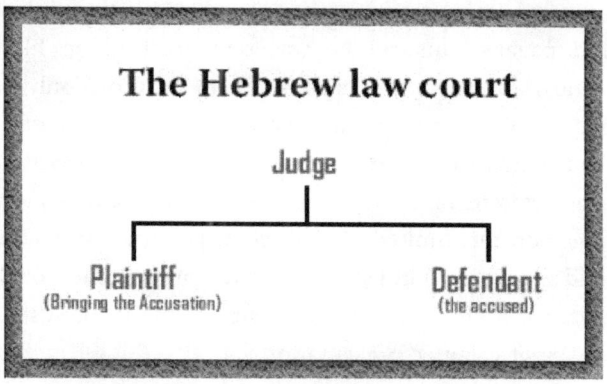

Wright then summarizes what this Jewish courtroom scene ultimately represents concerning God's act of judgment:

"What happens, then, when we put the covenantal meaning of God's righteousness together with the metaphorical level drawn from the law-court scene? God, of course, is the judge. Israel comes before him to plead her case against the wicked pagans who are oppressing her. She longs for her case to come to court, for God to hear it, and, in his own righteousness, to deliver her from her enemies. She longs, that is, to be justified, acquitted, vindicated."[41]

---

[40] Wright, Saint Paul, p. 97.
[41] Ibid., pp. 98-99.

Consider Mr. Wright's characterization of the Jewish courtroom and God's judiciary: first, if Mr. Wright were truly interested in investigating what Saint Paul really said about *the forensic nature of God's righteousness*, then it would have been extremely helpful for him to delve much more deeply into the third chapter of Romans. It was there (as mentioned earlier) that Paul cited King David who faced the tribunal of God where he confessed *his own* sin. Clearly, David wasn't thinking about "wicked pagans," instead he was only focused on his own wickedness, for he says: "...against Thee, and Thee only have *I* sinned." While it is true, that many O.T. texts speak of God's righteous vindication of His people against pagan nations, it is a gross overstatement to say that the model of God's judiciary converges on this limited idea *alone.* It certainly doesn't apply to David's confession in Psalm 51, or to Paul's citation of David in Romans 3. By this comparison alone, we should be suspicious about Wright's slanted presentation.

Second, as to the details of the Jewish courtroom, we must note that there are problems with Wright's presentation of this courtroom scene, both as a historical reality and as an earthly parallel to God's own judiciary. This is important because his errors yield serious misconceptions concerning the *contents of,* and the *actions taken,* in God's judiciary. A careful examination of Scripture shows that when Wright attempts to "unpack" the details of God's courtroom he managed to leave several items behind, resulting in a corrupted notion of *forensic*

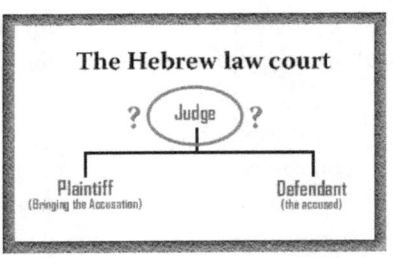

justification. Ultimately, these errors will help us to evaluate Wright's argument concerning the forensic aspect of God's righteousness. To do this, it will be necessary for us to examine several of the O.T. and N.T. texts that relate to our subject at hand. It will be especially needful for us to include N.T. revelation in this discussion, because without it, we are left with nothing but the tenebrous shadows of the Old Covenant, devoid of the light and substance of Christ Himself. In fact we can't expect to go to the O.T. Scriptures and successfully decipher *the forensic justification of Christ* apart from going to the very One to whom the O.T. points; or as Paul himself said:

> *Galatians 3:24: 24 Therefore the Law has become our tutor to lead us to Christ, so that we may be justified by faith.*

Thus, our examination of Christ's *forensic justification* will begin with the O.T. Scriptures, but then by the Law's *pedagogy* we will turn to Christ in the N.T. in order to come to a proper understanding of the full counsel of God – something that the Apostle Paul was dedicated to with his very life. By doing this, we are in fact imitating Paul's own wisdom as expressed in Galatians 3:24. What better way might a person come to discover *what Paul really meant and said?*

God's Courtroom in the O.T.

Wright's re-creation of the Jewish courtroom is one that manages to omit several significant texts of Scripture in both testaments. Particularly in the O.T., his omission of Deuteronomy chapters 17 and 19 is particularly troubling. By omitting these texts, Wright resultantly neglects the significant role of the *priests and witnesses,* and this is no small issue. Any student of the O.T. Scriptures should know right away that Wright's formula of *judge, plaintiff and defendant* fails to "unpack" all of the important components of the courtroom of God. Please examine the following text carefully:

Deuteronomy 19:15-20: 15 "A single witness shall not rise up against a man on account of any iniquity or any sin which he has committed; on the evidence of two or three witnesses a matter shall be confirmed. 16 "If a malicious witness rises up against a man to accuse him of wrongdoing, 17 then both the men who have the dispute shall stand before the Lord, before the priests and the judges who will be in office in those days. 18 "The judges shall investigate thoroughly, and if the witness is a false witness and he has accused his brother falsely, 19 then you shall do to him just as he had intended to do to his brother. Thus you shall purge the evil from among you. 20 "The rest will hear and be afraid, and will never again do such an evil thing among you."

The crucial nature of the *priesthood* is made even more obvious when we examine another Deuteronomic passage:

Deuteronomy 17:9, 12: 9 "So you shall come to the priests, the Levites, and to the judge there in those days, and inquire of them; they shall pronounce upon you the sentence of judgment...12 Now the man who acts presumptuously and will not heed the priest who stands to minister there before the Lord your God, or the judge, that man shall die. So you shall put away the evil from Israel." [NKJV]

These texts help us to see that Wright has not disclosed the true composition of the very judicial scene of which he writes, and such omissions as these lead to a defective concept of *forensic justification*. It is crucial that the reader understand that the Jewish courtroom consisted of the Lord *(Jehovah), the judges, priests, and witnesses,* as well as the *accused* and the *accuser:*

A casual reader might be tempted to ignore these omissions if it were not for the fact that these offices[42] actually foreshadow the very substance of Christ in His work of judgment and redemption. To think that we have any license to ignore any of these officers of the court is simply unspeakable. A timing chain in a car is quite small, and may seem unnecessary to the untrained eye, but just try taking it out of your engine – *you'll be going nowhere fast!* In a similar vein, Wright's omission of the priesthood and witnesses, in God's judiciary, grants him an artificial license to declare the following about the concept of God's justification of the sinner:

> *"If we use the language of the law court, it makes no sense whatever to say what the judge imputes, imparts, bequeaths, conveys or otherwise transfers his righteousness to either the plaintiff or the defendant. Righteousness is not an object, a substance or a gas which can be passed across the courtroom."*[43]

---

[42] Hebrews 10.
[43] Wright, Saint Paul, p. 98

> *"If we leave the notion of 'righteousness' as a law-court metaphor only, as so many have done in the past, this gives the impression of a legal transaction, a cold piece of business, almost a trick of thought performed by a God who is logical and correct but hardly one we would want to worship."*[44]

Wright contends, based upon the Old Testament's testimony alone, that there is no reason to believe that God's justification has anything to do with the imputation of His own righteousness. Of course, this argument of his remains entrenched in a *limited* presentation of the Old Covenant, devoid of any New Covenant revelation, and everything about this is problematic. Instead, the best way for us to investigate this matter is by examining the way in which the N.T. writers utilized the language of the O.T. judiciary. By this we can better understand the full substance of God's judiciary – not just as it stood in history, but as it previewed what was to come in the person of Jesus Christ. Therefore, there is no need for us to remain abandoned to the shadows of the O.T., without the aid and assistance of the N.T. In fact, as the disciples of Jesus Christ, it is our duty to conjoin our analysis of the O.T. to that of the N.T.

God's Courtroom in the N.T.

Wright's characterization of the Jewish courtroom must be held under the scrutiny of the whole counsel of God since the New Testament itself repeatedly spotlights the importance of God's judiciary in a number of ways. Especially when we consider the

---

[44] Ibid., 99.

The Forensic Context

writings of the Apostle Paul, Wright's primary focus of study, we find that he repeatedly depended on the O.T. standards of God's judiciary. To Timothy, Paul delivered the Deuteronomic standard as it applied to the church's officers:

1 Timothy 5:19: 19 Do not receive an accusation against an elder except ON THE BASIS OF TWO OR THREE WITNESSES.

As well, when writing to the church at Corinth, Paul invoked the standards of God's judiciary on several occasions. To those who were placing themselves in the position of judging him (1 Corinthians 4:1-4), Paul promised that the truth would be justly revealed by valid witnesses:

2 Corinthians 13:1: 1 This is the third time I am coming to you. EVERY FACT IS TO BE CONFIRMED BY THE TESTIMONY OF TWO OR THREE WITNESSES.[45]

And when dealing with the lawless conduct of the Corinthians, Paul again quoted from the Deuteronomic standard of judgment and discipline:

1 Corinthians 5:11-13: 11 ... I wrote to you not to associate with any so-called brother if he is an immoral person, or covetous, or an idolater, or a reviler, or a drunkard, or a swindler—not even to eat with such a one. 12 For what have I to do with judging outsiders? Do you not judge those who are within the church? 13 But those who are outside, God judges. REMOVE THE WICKED MAN FROM AMONG YOURSELVES.

---

[45] 2 Corinthians 13:10: 10 For this reason I am writing these things while absent, so that when present I need not use severity, in accordance with the authority which the Lord gave me for building up and not for tearing down.

Paul is clearly citing the O.T. when he speaks of the need for the testimony of *two or three witnesses*. As well, he is also upholding the O.T. punitive standard when he says, regarding the impenitent: *you shall purge the evil from among yourselves;* an expression that is used nine times in Deuteronomy to speak of the need for discipline against those who were found guilty of various transgressions. In all but one case, this disciplinary formula required the *death of the offender* (Deuteronomy 13:5; 17:7, 12; 21:21; 22:21-22, 24; 24:7). Therefore we must ask, *what is Paul calling for when he calls for the removal of the evil one?* The answer to this question gives us an important distinction between the Old Covenant and the New: Paul is not calling upon the Corinthians to execute the offender in question, instead he is following the example of Christ in the New Covenant of His blood. In the New Covenant, we find that the impenitent are to be removed from the fellowship of the church, not by death, but by excommunication so that in the mercy of the Gospel of Christ he may be led to repentance in the end. Such an action as this recognized that *Christ's role is much more than that of a Judge* and therefore it was for this reason that Paul had delivered the offender over to Satan that his spirit *might be saved in the day of the Lord Jesus.* This is a remarkably important distinction from the O.T. punitive standard and it helps us to see that Paul's real perspective, concerning God's judiciary, was entirely Christ centered. The same Gospel mercy that is seen in 1 Corinthians 5:1-13 is also clearly revealed in Matthew 18 where the Lord Jesus instructs His disciples concerning the New Covenant standards of discipline and mercy within the community of God's people:

The Forensic Context

Matthew 18:15-20: 15 "If your brother sins, go and show him his fault in private; if he listens to you, you have won your brother. 16 "But if he does not listen to you, take one or two more with you, so that BY THE MOUTH OF TWO OR THREE WITNESSES EVERY FACT MAY BE CONFIRMED. 17 "If he refuses to listen to them, tell it to the church; and if he refuses to listen even to the church, let him be to you as a Gentile and a tax collector. 18 "Truly I say to you, whatever you bind on earth shall have been bound in heaven; and whatever you loose on earth shall have been loosed in heaven. 19 "Again I say to you, that if two of you agree on earth about anything that they may ask, it shall be done for them by My Father who is in heaven. 20 "For where two or three have gathered together in My name, I am there in their midst."

This text clearly reflects the O.T. courtroom scene, in part, through its mention of the need for two or three witnesses for proper adjudication. However, as we have already noted, there is a stark difference between the New Covenant of Christ and the Old Covenant: *"...the man who acts presumptuously by not listening to the priest who stands there to serve the Lord your God, nor to the judge, that man shall die; thus you shall purge the evil from Israel"* (Deuteronomy 17:12). Now, in the New Covenant of Christ, execution is no longer the standard of discipline among the people of God. Instead, those who reject biblical counsel by *not listening to* the church; to its leaders; and ultimately to the Great High Priest of the church; are to be treated as outsiders to the community of God's people. Thus, instead of execution, we have excommunication, and this excommunication has one central design – the restoration of the offender through Gospel mercy:

Matthew 18:12-13: 12 "What do you think? If any man has a hundred sheep, and one of them has gone astray, does he not leave the ninety-nine on the mountains and go and search for the one that is straying? 13 "And if it turns out that he finds it, truly I say to you, he rejoices over it more than over the ninety-nine which have not gone astray.

What is often missed in many discussions concerning church discipline is this crucial fact: *the goal of all discipline is the salvation and restoration of the lost.* Thus, a more careful examination of texts like Matthew 18 shows us that Paul's standard of discipline was entirely grounded in the person and teaching of Christ. This is why the Apostle declared to the Corinthians: *"I have decided to deliver such a one to Satan for the destruction of his flesh, that his spirit may be saved in the day of the Lord Jesus."* Whatever one might want to say about Paul's perspective on God's judiciary, this conclusion must be clearly embraced: Paul's understanding regarding the Old Covenant judiciary could never be divorced from the One to whom the Old Testament Scriptures pointed.

When carefully compared, both Matthew 18:15-20 and 1 Corinthians 5:1-13 clearly show that the O.T. judiciary is in fact a foreshadowing of Christ Himself who is the supreme *Judge, Priest, and Witness* within the reality of the New Covenant. Ultimately, the repeated testimony of Scripture reveals Christ's fulfillment of each office, as:

1. The supreme Judge (Acts 17:31, John 5:22, 27).

2. The Great High Priest (Ephesians 5:1-2, Hebrews 2:17).

3. The True and Faithful Witness (2 Corinthians 1:18-23, Revelation 3:14):[46]

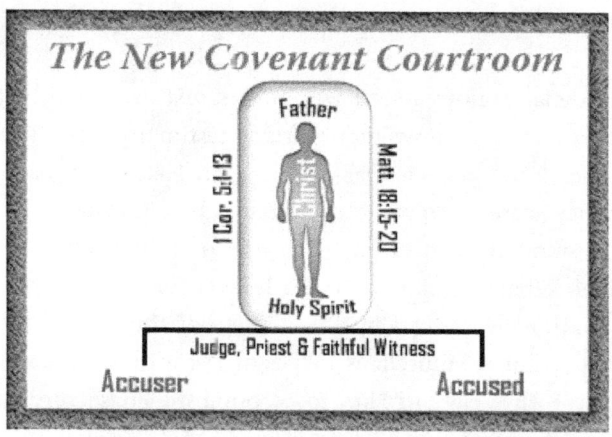

I must also remind the reader that while our emphasis has thus far focused upon the offices of judge and priest, we must not minimize the importance of Christ's role as witness. For many, it may be more obvious to focus exclusively upon the *judicial* and *priestly* offices, however we see that Christ's role as a *witness* is equally crucial:

> *John 8:12-18: 12 ... "I am the light of the world; he who follows Me shall not walk in the darkness, but shall have the light of life." 13 So the Pharisees said to Him, "You are testifying about Yourself; Your testimony is not true." 14 Jesus answered and said to them, "Even if I testify about Myself, My testimony is true, for I know where I came from and where I am going; but you do not know where I come from or where I am going. 15 "You judge according to the flesh; I am not judging anyone. 16 "But even if I do judge, My judgment is true; for I*

---

[46] Christ is called, by name, "The Amen, the faithful and true Witness": Revelation 3:14 "And to the angel of the church in Laodicea write: The Amen, the faithful and true Witness, the Beginning of the creation of God, says this..."

am not alone in it, but I and the Father who sent Me. 17 "Even in your law it has been written that the testimony of two men is true. 18 "I am He who testifies about Myself, and the Father who sent Me testifies about Me."

The judicial notions found within this text are unmistakable. The Jews were arguing that Christ's testimony [*martureis*][47] was invalid because He was speaking on His own behalf, and thus they were charging that Christ was failing to fulfill the lawful standard concerning the use of witnesses within a tribunal. What they did not understand is that Christ's ministry was continually ratified by the witness of the Father, by the witness of Christ Himself, as well as by the witness of the works that the Father gave to Him to accomplish. These very truths were communicated by Christ earlier in John's Gospel:

John 5:22, 30-37: 22 "For not even the Father judges anyone, but He has given all judgment to the Son...30 "I can do nothing on My own initiative. As I hear, I judge; and My judgment is just, because I do not seek My own will, but the will of Him who sent Me. 31 "If I alone testify about Myself, My testimony is not true. 32 "There is another who testifies of Me, and I know that the testimony which He gives about Me is true. 33 "You have sent to John, and he has testified to the truth. 34 "But the testimony which I receive is not from man, but I say these things so that you may be saved. 35 "He was the lamp that was burning and was shining and you were willing to rejoice for a while in his light. 36 "But the testimony which I have is greater than the testimony of John; for the works which the Father has given Me to accomplish—the very works that I do—testify about Me, that the Father has sent Me. 37 "And the Father who sent Me, He has testified

---

[47] In Deuteronomy chapters 17 and 19 [LXX] the Greek word *martureō* is employed as in John chapters 5 and 8. The deuteronomic standard of two or three witnesses is clearly in view in both cases.

The Forensic Context

of Me. You have neither heard His voice at any time nor seen His form."

The full counsel of God consistently yields the clear disclosure of Christ's threefold office as *judge, priest, and witness,* revealing the Savior's *justice, mercy, and veracity*:

1. Justice: He has all authority to *judge* the living and the dead.

2. Mercy: He has all authority to grant mercy and forgiveness as our *High Priest*.

3. Veracity: He has the authority to speak as *"the Amen, the true and Faithful Witness"* seeing that He speaks with the testimony of the Father, as well as with the testimony of the works that had been given to Him to perform. In the final judgment of the nations, Christ will not only separate and judge the nations as the sheep and the goats, but He will also testify as the omniscient witness of their life and conduct, unto eternal bliss or unto eternal condemnation.

As an Apostle of Jesus Christ, Paul's understanding of forensic justification was deeply embedded in the Savior's instruction and example. The Lord was Paul's *Judge, Priest, and Witness* and such realities must not be ignored when we consider Paul's mention of *justification as a forensic term.* All of these texts are crucial if we really wish to discover what Paul really said and meant when he spoke of forensic justification. Whether we are considering the context of the N.T. church, or the Son's final judgment of the nations – Christ has preeminence over everything:

Ephesians 1:20-23: 20 which He brought about in Christ, when He raised Him from the dead, and seated Him at His right hand in the heavenly places, 21 far above all rule and authority and power and dominion, and every name that is named, not only in this age, but also in the one to come. 22 And He put all things in subjection under His feet, and gave Him as head over all things to the church, 23 which is His body, the fullness of Him who fills all in all.

Now that we have examined several texts from the Old and New Testament Scriptures, we must now revisit Mr. Wright's development of the O.T. courtroom, along with his attempt to relate it to the New Covenant reality in Christ. Recall his earlier statement:

"If we use the language of the law court, it makes no sense whatever to say what the judge imputes, imparts, bequeaths, conveys or otherwise transfers his righteousness to either the plaintiff or the defendant. Righteousness is not an object, a substance or a gas which can be passed across the courtroom."[48]

For the sake of argument, I wish to agree with what Mr. Wright says in the above paragraph. Clearly it is true that the O.T. courtroom scene supplies no evidence or precedence of any human judge *imputing, imparting, bequeathing, conveying or transferring his righteousness to either the plaintiff or the defendant.* While this thought might appear to have some value, it must be noted that as an *argument of omission* it supplies us with no real point that could be deemed as being useful. If anything, it is a dangerous form of thinking. By using such an argument of omission, we could very quickly concoct some additional bad doctrines. Notice just how meaningless the argument of omission is in the following examples:

---

[48] Wright, Saint Paul, p. 98.

The Forensic Context

1. There is no O.T. courtroom precedent of a human judge removing the death penalty by granting the mercy of forgiveness - but this did not stop the Savior from doing so (John 8:1-12).

2. Nor is there any O.T. courtroom precedent for a single human witness offering testimony, along with the audible witness of God and the visible witness of a perfect righteousness, but this is exactly what Christ did (John 5).

3. Nor is there an O.T. courtroom precedent of a sinner imputing his guilt onto any of the officers of the court, whether a judge, priest, or witness; and yet Paul teaches us that Christ became a curse for us (Gal. 3:13).

4. Nor is there any O.T. courtroom precedent for the priest offering himself as a sacrificial substitute on behalf of the guilty, but this is exactly what Christ accomplished in His own substitutionary sacrifice (2 Corinthians 5:21).

5. And there is certainly no O.T. courtroom precedent for a punished officer of the court to die and rise again on the third day – but again – this is exactly what our Savior did to the glory of the Father!

The great danger of the argument of omission should be evident. If Mr. Wright can grant himself permission to deny the concept of imputed righteousness by his concocted omissions, then what might be done with the five aforementioned works of Christ? Wright's reasoning is quite dangerous, and those who try to employ the *argument of omission* prove precious little, except perhaps their own ignorance about what is needed to construct a meaningful argument. But Wright would have his readers to try in vain to resolve the clarity of Christ's full work and mission by searching in the shadows of O.T. revelation *alone*. It is here that I must say that Wright's *modern use of the*

Bible is innovative for sure; but it also exceeds the boundaries of credulity.

Wright's version of the Jewish courtroom becomes the bad foundation for his own construct concerning God's justification of the sinner, in Christ. It is as though the reader is obligated to avoid all New Testament revelation, while remaining imprisoned in a courtroom that is devoid of any *priestly advocacy, or faithful witnesses*, so that Wright can then say: *"To imagine the defendant somehow receiving the judge's righteousness is simply a category mistake. That is not how the language works."* In reality, it is Wright who has erred at several levels by limiting the O.T. Scriptures while ignoring the teachings of Christ and the Apostle Paul, in his attempt to define justification. Thus Wright's characterization of God's judiciary is without merit, and the lexical, historical, grammatical, and category mistakes are all his. As well, Wright's use of the statement, concerning God's righteousness not being "a gas which can be passed across the courtroom," is rather *clownish*. Has there ever been a serious theologian in human history who has defended the doctrine of imputed righteousness *in such terms?* When men haven't the acumen to produce a cohesive argument, they will often dig from the dregs of *ad hominem* attacks. Thus, we are led to assume that those who believe in the doctrine of imputed righteousness are guilty of reducing the gift of God's justification *to an ether.*

But it is Wright's unbiblical courtroom that clearly endangers the office and work of Christ. How exactly is it that Paul was able to say that Christ, who knew no sin, became sin on our behalf, if this was not accomplished by means of *imputation?*

The Forensic Context

By nullifying the concept of *imputed righteousness*, in the judiciary of God, Wright also calls into doubt the veracity of imputed guilt. If we truly desire to embrace what Saint Paul really said, we must call to mind 2 Corinthians 5:21 which clearly teaches that Christ bore our sins so that we, by imputation, would bear His righteousness:

> *2 Corinthians 5:21 He made Him who knew no sin to be sin on our behalf, that we might become the righteousness of God in Him.*

The Savior was pierced through and crushed for our iniquities.[49] To say that He was made sin on our behalf is to recognize that Christ, who knew no sin, was treated as though He was guilty of our transgressions. That is, our sins were *credited* to Him while His righteousness was *credited* to us:

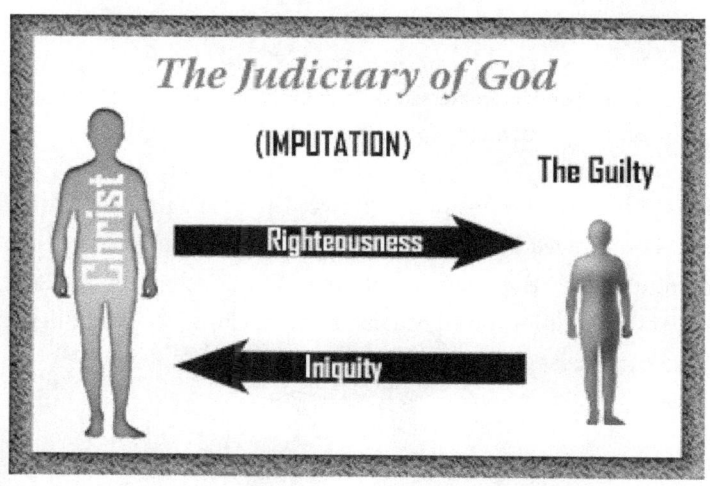

---

[49] Isaiah 53:5.

This simple concept of imputation is crucial. It informs us that as the sinner is *in Christ* so it is the case that Christ remains sinless. Only through the imputation of our guilt to Christ can it be said that He was condemned for our sin and guilt. As well, the principle of imputation also informs us that the redeemed remain sinful, while at the same time being declared *the righteousness of God – in Christ.* He *received the penalty of our sin* (through imputation) so that we (through imputation), would be *credited* with His righteousness. Calvin understands the importance of Paul's mention of our being *in Christ*, when he said:

> "There can be no doubt that he who is taught to seek righteousness out of himself does not previously possess it in himself. This is most clearly declared by the Apostle, when he says, that he who knew no sin was made an expiatory victim for sin, that we might be made the righteousness of God in him (2 Cor. 5:21). You see that our righteousness is not in ourselves, but in Christ; that the only way in which we become possessed of it is by being made partakers with Christ, since with him we possess all riches." [50]

It is this small prepositional phrase "in Him" and "in Christ" that is employed by Saint Paul no less than 117 times in order to communicate the nature of our relationship with God. However, without the righteous merit of Christ we could never have such access to the Father:

---

[50] John Calvin, Institutes of the Christian Religion, vol. 1, The Library of Christian Classics, Vol XX, ed. John T. McNeill, trans., Ford Lewis Battles (The Westminster Press), p. 753.

The Forensic Context

Ephesians 2:18 for through Him[51] we both have our access in one Spirit to the Father.

Such a description of our *relational* access to the Father comes after the Apostle's thorough presentation of the Christian's position *in Christ:*

> Ephesians 1:1 (in Christ Jesus); 1:3 (in Christ); 1:6 (in the Beloved); 1:7 (in Him); 1:9 (in Him); 1:10 (in Christ); 1:11 (in Him); 1:12 (in Christ); 1:13 (in Him 2xs); 2:5 (in Christ); 2:6 (with Him 2xs, in Christ Jesus) 2:7 (in Christ Jesus); 2:10 (in Christ Jesus); 2:13 (in Christ Jesus); 2:15 (in Himself).

Paul's frequent references to our being *in Christ* reminds us of the fact that without Christ's righteous covering[52] we could never have such a relationship with God. In other words, having a relationship with God is synonymous with being *in Christ* who is our righteous Advocate and Priest. Yet despite these crucial truths, Wright continues to press his point about how justification is something quite different. It does not entail the thought of imputation, nor does it include the notion of having a relationship with God.[53] This logic of his then leads him to make this strange admission in his book:

> "Despite a long tradition to the contrary, the problem Paul addresses in Galatians is not the question of how precisely someone becomes a Christian, or attains to a relationship with God. (I'm not even sure

---

[51] Ephesians 2:13 But now in Christ Jesus you who formerly were far off have been brought near by the blood of Christ.

[52] Galatians 3:27 For all of you who were baptized into Christ have clothed yourselves with Christ.

[53] Wright, Saint Paul, p. 119.

Indeed, Has Paul Really Said?

how Paul would express, in Greek, our notion of 'relationship with God', but we'll leave that aside.)"[54]

Though Wright's final comment is parenthetical, it is not any less significant or troubling. Wright insists that he is not sure how Paul would express the notion of having a relationship with God. Statements like these reveal a strange desperation in his effort to transform justification from that of soteriology to ecclesiology. However, central to Paul's Gospel message is this reality, that alienated sinners can have a relationship with God *in Christ*. Thus, one of Paul's chief arguments is that we now have peace with God *in and through Christ* (Romans 5:1, 8:1), having access to Him through the Spirit (Eph. 2:18). How can the guilty and condemned sinner have a relationship with the supreme Judge of the Universe? – by taking refuge in the Righteous One who stands in God's judiciary as our Great High Priest. Only *in Christ* is the judiciary of God transformed into a place that is devoid of condemnation. Yet, despite this reality, Wright argues for a different picture of God's judiciary, as we saw earlier in this chapter:

"If we leave the notion of 'righteousness' as a law-court metaphor only, as so many have done in the past, this gives the impression of a legal transaction, a cold piece of business, almost a trick of thought performed by a God who is logical and correct but hardly one we would want to worship."[55]

The irony of Wright's criticisms must not go unnoticed here. *First*, his complaint against those who would reduce the lexical

---

[54] Ibid., p. 120.
[55] Ibid., 99.

analysis of *the righteousness of God* to that of a monolithic-forensic idea is *incredible*. Wright's own labors to reduce God's righteousness to the monolithic notion of *covenant faithfulness* makes him guilty of the same categorical mistake. Thus, it would seem that Mr. Wright is willing to rebuke those who err through a limited lexical analysis, unless that limited lexical analysis upholds his own definitions. *Second*, the very basis of Mr. Wright's complaint about the forensic context of God's righteousness is the result of his own doing. To him, the judiciary of God is a cold and logical place, but this is due to his own omission of the priestly office as a preview to Christ in the O.T., and as revealed in Christ in the N.T. We can agree that without our glorious High Priest, God's courtroom is reduced to a dark and merciless chamber. Calvin is right when he says:

"...being reconciled by the righteousness of Christ, God becomes, instead of a judge, an indulgent Father."[56]

The problem is not that the law-court metaphor yields a *trick of thought performed by a God who is logical and correct but hardly one we would want to worship.* The real problem is that Mr. Wright has performed his own *trick of thought* whereby he has left the O.T. judiciary without the merciful and gracious intercession of our righteous Advocate[57] and Faithful Witness. Frankly speaking it is Wright's own law-court, devoid of the Savior's propitious representation, that leaves us with a *cold piece of business*.

The courtroom of the Old Covenant has but one design - to point us to the supreme court of Jesus Christ. All men will

---

[56] Calvin, Institutes, p. 725.
[57] John 10, 17.

appear in God's courtroom someday, and they will all answer to Him. To those who rejected Him in this life, they will be found guilty, not by two or three human witnesses, but by the triune witness established by the Son, along with the Father and the Holy Spirit.[58] But to those who trusted Christ in this life they will face Him in His priestly office as the One who is the great *Advocate, intercessor,* and *sacrificial substitute* for His sheep (John 17). It is in this courtroom of Christ that the believer is *now* no longer condemned (Romans 8:1), because they *have been justified* through faith in Christ (Romans 5:1). Our righteous advocate (1 John 2:1) bore our sins so that we would be justified by His righteousness:

Isaiah 53:11: 11 As a result of the anguish of His soul, He will see it and be satisfied; By His knowledge the Righteous One, My Servant, will justify the many, As He will bear their iniquities.

This is the great work of our Savior, the Lord Jesus Christ. To the reader I offer this warning: do not let anyone diminish the importance of these truths for you. Simply put, if you're a Christian, your soul depends upon these great truths!

---

[58] John 16:7-11.

Chapter 3

The Righteousness of God and Paul's Apostleship

Up to this point we have considered Mr. Wright's presentation of his lexical as well as his historical/forensic understanding of God's righteousness. His argument has relied heavily on approaches that either avoid or redact the Scriptures.

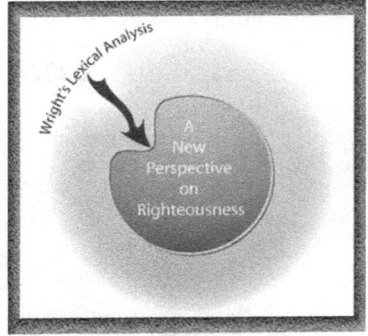

Lexically speaking, his presentation of a new perspective on righteousness has required an approach which reduces the semantic domain of *righteous/righteousness* to one single band of thought – covenant faithfulness. And as we saw in the previous chapter, Wright's attempt to "unpack" the Jewish courtroom scene was vastly incomplete, leaving us without the adequate tools to come to terms with what the Bible teaches us concerning God's work of justifying the sinner. Such omissions

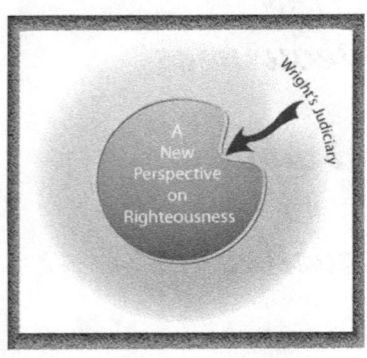

as these leave us without the proper previews of Christ's work of justifying the ungodly[59] while He Himself bears their sins as their sacrificial substitute.[60] The unified testimony of Holy Writ is that the Savior is the Christian's *Priestly Advocate, Intercessor,* and *Substitute,*

---

[59] Romans 4:5 But to the one who does not work, but believes in Him who justifies the ungodly, his faith is reckoned as righteousness,
[60] Hebrews 9:28.

and this is why the believer can stand in confidence when He returns.⁶¹ The great danger that we face in all of this is that Mr. Wright is effectively doing much more than warping the meaning of a single word or phrase. His methodologies ultimately infringe upon several truths concerning the person and work of the Lord Jesus Christ. It is here that I do not hesitate to say that Wright's courtroom scene is clearly a Christless one, devoid of any *preview of His Advocacy on our behalf.* By these procedures of his, the reader is sadly turned away from the substance of Christ in order to be abandoned to the O.T. shadows of Mosaic law - *and a limited perspective of the Mosaic law at that.* Such a Christless judiciary as this *is indeed a new perspective on Paul - but it is a grotesquely wrong one.*

But now we must move to our third point of analysis which will deal with *Paul's Apostleship.* It is here that we will examine how Wright seeks to transform the background and beliefs of Paul so that the reader is advised to retool his understanding of the Apostle's every mention of *righteousness and justification.* Wright is convinced that Paul was a Shammaite⁶² Pharisee (rather than being a student of Gamaliel). The import of this argument of his is very significant because, in this new system of thought, the righteousness of God is to be seen as God's covenant faithfulness as worked out in the final *eschaton*, such that the concept of justification is, principally, an end-times concept. Wright even summarizes what he believed was Paul's

---

⁶¹ 1 John 2:28.

⁶² "Resurrection, for Saul of Tarsus as a Shammaite Pharisee, was bound up with the national hope of Israel. Israel would be raised to life, while the Gentiles received their punishment." Wright, Saint Paul, p. 141.

Shammaite coloration regarding *the righteousness of God* and *justification*:

> *"Put these two (justification and eschatology) together, and what happens? 'Justification', the great moment of salvation seen in terms of the fulfillment of the covenant and in terms of the last great law-court scene, would thus also be eschatological: it would be the final fulfillment of Israel's long-cherished hope. Putting it another way, the Jewish eschatological hope was hope for justification, for God to vindicate his people at last."*[63]

It is indeed true that the concept of the sinner's justification looks to an eschatological climax; after all, the final scenes of judgment in the book of Revelation remind us that God's final redemption of His people will reveal the fruit of His work of justification. However, Wright's emphasis on this supposed Pauline-Shammaite eschatology propels him to declare that the Christian's present justification is evidentiary in nature, and not salvific:

> *"Justification is not how someone becomes a Christian. It is the declaration that they have become a Christian."*[64]

> *"It is not 'how you become a Christian', so much as 'how you can tell who is a member of the covenant family.'"*[65]

In view of his argument, and for the sake of simplicity, we could think of justification in terms of *visible evidence alone*. Thus, the believer's visible participation in the community of the church is the *present evidence* of the believer's *future justification*:

---

[63] Ibid., p. 34.
[64] Ibid., p. 125.
[65] Ibid., p. 122.

"'Justification' in the first century was not about how someone might establish a relationship with God. It was about God's eschatological definition, both future and present, of who was, in fact, a member of his people. In Sanders' terms, it was not so much about 'getting in', or indeed about 'staying in', as about 'how you could tell who was in'. In standard Christian theological language, it wasn't so much about soteriology as about ecclesiology; not so much about salvation as about the church."[66]

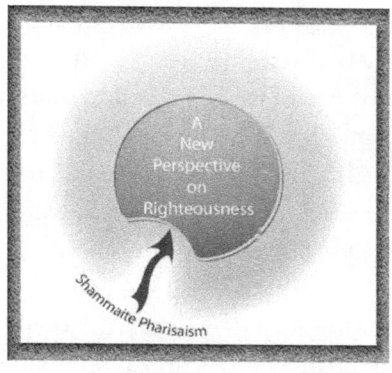

Wright's mantra of a supposed Pauline-Shammaite eschatology is the third branch in his development which seeks to revise the historic concept of *justification by faith*.[67] This is perhaps the most awkward aspect of his book as it reveals a kind of exegetical desperation on his part to transform what Paul really meant and said. To do this, Wright seeks to revise the language of Paul by making some gargantuan changes to the Apostle's past:

> "Where does Saul of Tarsus belong on this map of first-century Pharisaic belief and activity? In one of the speeches in Acts (22:3) he claims that Gamaliel had been one of his teachers. This, coupled with other evidence from the epistles, has led some scholars to suppose that he was a Hillelite before his conversion. This simply cannot be the case - unless all the evidence of his persecuting activity is a later fabrication, which seems highly unlikely. The Gamaliel of Acts 5 would not have approved of the stoning of Stephen. He would never

---

[66] Ibid., p. 119.
[67] Ibid., pp. 117-18.

have dreamed of riding off to Damascus to haul Christians into prison and to death." [68]

"Saul's persecution of the church, and the word 'zeal' with which he describes it, puts him firmly on the map of a certain type of first-century Judaism...it reveals Saul of Tarsus not just as a Jew, but as a Pharisee; not just as a Pharisee, but as a Shammaite Pharisee; not just, perhaps, as a Shammaite Pharisee, but as one of the strictest of the sect." [69]

It is by this paragraph, and others like it, that Wright presents the Apostle Paul as one who has been misunderstood in terms of his pharisaical upbringing, and that this has falsely skewed our understanding of the Apostle's overall message about *the righteousness of God*. Because Paul used the word *zeal* to describe his former manner of life, Wright concludes that Paul was not so much a student of Gamaliel (Gamaliel the grandson of Hillel), but instead he was a Shammaite Pharisee. And there you have it, another unsubstantiated *QED!* Apparently Mr. Wright believes that being a zealous Jew can only mean bloodshed and violence despite the fact that Christ Himself was *consumed with zeal for His Father's house (John 2:17)*, but not according to Mr. Wright's characterization:

"...for the first-century Jew 'zeal' was something you did with a knife."[70]

Our Savior was consumed with zeal, and yet who would assume that He committed violence?;[71] or who would dare conclude that He was associated with the Shammaites simply because He

---

[68] Ibid., pp. 29-30.
[69] Ibid., p. 26.
[70] Ibid., p. 27.
[71] Isaiah 53:9.

was zealous in His ministry to the Father? Clearly, such queries would be deemed ludicrous by most, and yet, Wright's logic isn't much more sophisticated than this. Sadly, such oversimplified statements like these characterize Wright's argumentative method. Jewish zeal did often mean violence (as Paul testified), but it didn't *necessarily denote* such violence; nor did it *necessarily denote* that such zeal made a person a Shammaite Pharisee. Strangely enough, by Wright's unsubstantiated interpretation concerning Paul's *former zeal as a Jew*, we are now expected to rethink all of Paul's writings. Sadly, with this interpretive protocol in place, the writings of Paul are now subjected to the coloration of a Shammaite-Pharisaic tradition, and those who wish to understand the meanings of Paul must now consult the decoder ring of the Mishnah as well as the intertestamental writings of the apocrypha and the Pseudepigrapha; and all of this impacts, once again, his presentation of *the righteousness of God.* It is to this end that Mr. Wright has done more than just question Paul's academic pedigree – he has infused non-canonical writings into Holy Writ itself. As students of Scripture, we must be careful to see if there is any merit in Wright's argument from God's Word at all. In this section, we will examine two points of interest. First, we will examine what Paul said about his Pharisaic pedigree and second, we will consider if his past impacted his life as an Apostle of Jesus Christ. Once again, a careful study of these matters will aid us in understanding what Saint Paul really said.

Paul's Pharisaic Pedigree

We begin by looking at what it is that Paul says concerning his own pedigree as a Pharisee. To do this we will begin with Acts 22 (which Wright himself references) in order to see what we can learn about Paul's past. The context of Paul's address in Acts 22 is one of hostility, for Paul was nearly killed by the "violence of the mob" of Jews who sought his death.[72] Thus, when Paul spoke to his audience, there is a sense in which he was looking in the mirror of what he himself was before he was saved by grace in Christ.[73] This is the repeated testimony of the Apostle – that he too was a violent persecutor of the church. It is this same testimony that he also offered before King Agrippa in Acts 26:

| Acts 22:4-5: 4 "I persecuted this Way to the death, binding and delivering into prisons both men and women, 5 "as also the high priest bears me witness, and all the council of the elders, from whom I also received letters to the brethren, and went to Damascus to bring in chains even those who were there to Jerusalem to be punished." NKJV | Acts 26:10-11: 10 "This I also did in Jerusalem, and many of the saints I shut up in prison, having received authority from the chief priests; and when they were put to death, I cast my vote against them. 11 "And I punished them often in every synagogue and compelled them to blaspheme; and being exceedingly enraged against them, I persecuted them even to foreign cities." NKJV |

---

[72] Acts 21.

[73] "In his conciliation he went to the limit and puts himself by the side of the mob in their zeal for the law, mistaken as they were about him." *Word Pictures in the New Testament*, Archibald Thomas Robertson, (Baker Book House, Grand Rapids Michigan, 1930), p. 387.

Acts chapters 22 and 26 leave the reader with little doubt concerning the *extent* of Saul's zeal in persecuting the Way. In the presence of King Agrippa, Paul said that he had been *furiously enraged* at the saints, that is to say, he was *nearly insane* with hatred for Christians.[74] Paul's zeal was taken to its greatest possible extreme, and as such, he excelled above others in his desire to exterminate the followers of the way.[75] This he did after the pattern of the O.T. judiciary, believing that the followers of the Way were heretics who stood condemned:

Christians Were Viewed as Heretics: The historic standard for dealing with false teachers was that of stoning: *Deuteronomy 13:5,10: 5 "But that prophet or that dreamer of dreams shall be put to death, because he has counseled rebellion against the Lord your God who brought you from the land of Egypt and redeemed you from the house of slavery, to seduce you from the way in which the Lord your God commanded you to walk. So you shall purge the evil from among you....10 "So you shall stone him to death because he has sought to seduce you from the Lord your God who brought you out from the land of Egypt, out of the house of slavery."*

Christians Were Condemned by the Sanhedrin: In Paul's day, the judicial authority of the nation was principally vested in the council of the Sanhedrin of Jerusalem, a council of 70 elders comprised of the high priests (the serving high priest and former high priests), Sadducees, Pharisees and scribes. It is this very Council of the Sanhedrin, along with the high priest, that Paul served when he sought the imprisonment and death of the followers of Christ: Acts

---

[74] G. *emmainomai*: "...to be so furiously angry with someone as to be almost out of one's mind." Louw, J. P., & Nida, E. A. (1996, c1989). *Greek-English lexicon of the New Testament : Based on semantic domains* (electronic ed. of the 2nd edition.) (1:761). New York: United Bible societies.

[75] Philippians 3:4-6: 4 ... If anyone else has a mind to put confidence in the flesh, I far more: 5 circumcised the eighth day, of the nation of Israel, of the tribe of Benjamin, a Hebrew of Hebrews; as to the Law, a Pharisee; 6 as to zeal, a persecutor of the church; as to the righteousness which is in the Law, found blameless.

26:10 "...not only did I lock up many of the saints in prisons, *having received authority from the chief priests*,[76] but also when they were being put to death I cast my vote against them."

Armed with such authority, Paul acted on what he believed to be the will of God – *to persecute the followers of Christ*. Thus, when Stephen was being crushed to death for preaching the Gospel of Jesus Christ, Saul stood there over his crushed and dying body, being in hearty agreement with his executors:

Acts 7:56-8:1: 56 and he [Stephen] said, "Behold, I see the heavens opened up and the Son of Man standing at the right hand of God." 57 But they cried out with a loud voice, and covered their ears, and they rushed upon him with one impulse. 58 And when they had driven him out of the city, they began stoning him, and the witnesses laid aside their robes at the feet of a young man named Saul. 59 And they went on stoning Stephen as he called upon the Lord and said, "Lord Jesus, receive my spirit!" 60 And falling on his knees, he cried out with a loud voice, "Lord, do not hold this sin against them!" And having said this, he fell asleep. 1 And Saul was in hearty agreement with putting him to death. And on that day a great persecution arose against the church in Jerusalem; and they were all scattered throughout the regions of Judea and Samaria, except the apostles.

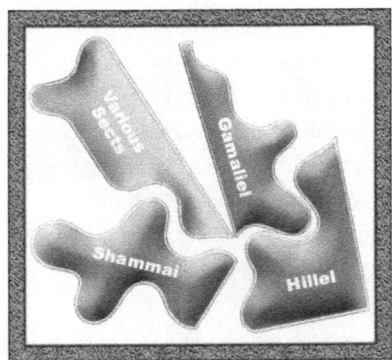

Paul's familiarity with the Jewish courtroom was

---

[76] Italics mine. Paul's authority was derived from the deuteronomic standard already mentioned earlier: Deuteronomy 17:12 "And the man who acts presumptuously by not listening to the priest ... nor to the judge, that man shall die; thus you shall purge the evil from Israel."

certainly extensive. His application of the judicial texts of the O.T. granted him the license to pursue what he believed to be a heretical sect that was leading the Jews astray: *Christianity*. It is no wonder that Paul spoke with such openness to his audiences about his former manner of life, after all his Jewish background was well known by many. Even his testimony in Acts 26 reveals that King Agrippa was one who had deep familiarity with the customs and questions of the Jews:

> Acts 26:2-3: 2 "In regard to all the things of which I am accused by the Jews, I consider myself fortunate, King Agrippa, that I am about to make my defense before you today; 3 especially because you are an expert in all customs and questions among the Jews; therefore I beg you to listen to me patiently."

This familiarity of Paul's listeners is especially seen in Acts 22, where Paul was able to speak to them in familiar terms, not only regarding his own zealous background, but he spoke to them in their own Hebrew dialect. In each case (Acts 22 & 26), Paul knew that his audience would comprehend the details of his testimony as those who were deeply familiar with the customs and traditions of the Jews. Therefore, all of Paul's hearers *would certainly know if there was something missing concerning his personal testimony as a Pharisee*. With this in mind, consider the following comparison of Acts 22 & 26:

Acts 22:3 "I am indeed a Jew, born in Tarsus of Cilicia, but brought up in this city at the feet of Gamaliel, taught according to the strictness of our fathers' law, and was zealous toward God as you all are today."	Acts 26:4-5: 4 "My manner of life from my youth, which was spent from the beginning among my own nation at Jerusalem, all the Jews know. 5 "They knew me from the first, if they were willing to testify, that according to the strictest sect of our religion I lived a Pharisee."

Indeed, Has Paul Really Said?

Paul The Shammaite Pharisee

Whenever Paul offered his testimony regarding his zealous persecution of the church, at no time did he credit his reasoning to some supposed Shammaite influence. Therefore, when Wright insists that Paul was a Shammaite, he does so on the basis of an implicit argument alone. But of course, to say that Paul never admitted to being a Shammaite is in fact an *argument of omission*, therefore it is imperative that I remind the reader that the only school of influence that he does mention is that of *Gamaliel*. Notice that Paul did not say that Gamaliel was *one of his instructors*, instead he declared that he received training *at the feet* [*para tous podas*] of this historic teacher of Israel. This familiar expression is an unmistakable recognition of submission, devotion, and adoration (Matt. 15:30; Luke 8:35, 8:41, 17:16; Acts 4:35). Strangely, Wright omits this crucial expression in his book, thus opening the door for this false characterization of the Apostle: *"he [Paul] claims that Gamaliel had been one of his teachers."* One would have to wonder by what authority Wright is able to reduce the bold assertions of an Apostle to that of a *mere* claim - *even a false claim*. The text gives us no reason to assume that Paul had any devotion to any other school than that of Gamaliel. In fact, Paul's stated devotion to Gamaliel should remind us that for a first century Jewish student, devotion to one's Rabbi was chief among all earthly relationships:

> "The Rabbis required from their pupils the most absolute reverence, surpassing even the honour felt for parents. 'Let thine esteem for thy

friend border upon thy respect for thy teacher, and respect for thy teacher on reverence for God.'"[77]

To say that Paul had some brief and transitory devotion to Gamaliel, such that he was just *one of his instructors* (and a lesser one, according to Wright), is an utterly foreign imposition to the biblical text, as well as to first century history. Contrarily, Paul sat as a devoted student *at the very feet of Gamaliel*. For anyone to infuse another source into Paul's religious pedigree is to deny the explicit confession of the Apostle Paul himself. As to the matter of Paul's zealous rage against the Christian community, there is an important piece of information that he gave when speaking to King Agrippa in Acts 26:

Acts 26:9 "So then, I thought to myself that I had to do many things hostile to the name of Jesus of Nazareth."

When Paul says "I thought to myself" - the language of *self-inquiry* is unmistakable [G. *Egō...edoxa emautō > I reasoned to myself*]. The force of the pronoun [*Egō - I*] plus the reflexive pronoun [*emautō - myself*] reveals that Paul had *decided for himself* that he had a divine obligation to pursue Christians to the death, based upon the authority of the law[78] and armed with the authority of the chief priest. This is Paul's most explicit description of what led him to his zealous and violent persecution of the way. In light of the detail that he supplies concerning his decision, it would seem to be rather odd to

---

[77] The Literature of the Jewish People in the Time of Jesus, 2nd Division Volume I, Emil Schürer, (Hendrickson Publishers, 1995) p. 317. There are several such expressions in the Mishnah, most of which come during a later time in the development of the recorded Mishnah. It should be evident by this tradition that such convictions found their roots in the ancient Pharisaic schools established long before the Apostle Paul.

[78] Philippians 3:6 as to zeal, a persecutor of the church; as to the righteousness which is in the Law, found blameless.

charge Paul with being the member of a violent sect. If he were a member of such a group, then his pursuit of violence would

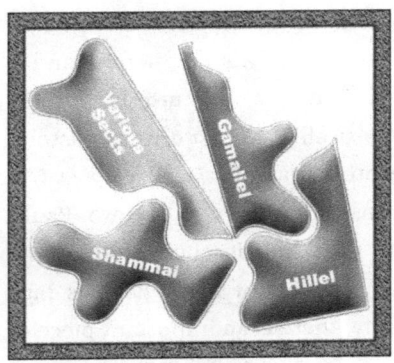

have been a simple matter of complicity with the sect, not a unique decision mulled over by an individual. However, as a follower of Gamaliel, this confession harmonizes very well. Taking Paul at his own word, the causation of his zealous violence came not from his complicity with a group, instead, Paul's decision to use violence came from his own conviction as an independent choice. This would comport with the idea that Paul had distanced himself from the more moderate elements within the school of Gamaliel. However, in pointing out these things we must also remember that whether we are speaking of the followers of Gamaliel or Shammai, care must be taken not to assume too much about these groups, especially during the growing persecution of the church. It should be evident when reading the Gospel accounts themselves, that the various Jewish sects were in a constant state of flux, especially during the life of Christ and the early church. Even the Sadducees and Pharisees found a basis of unity through their mutual hatred of Christ – something that would seem impossible in view of their historic hostility towards one another. Because of these important factors, care must be taken when considering the social dynamics between the various sects of the Pharisees and the Sadducees during this tumultuous time. What we know for certain, by the authority of God's Word, is that Paul had no hesitation to mention his training under Gamaliel when confessing his intense zeal as a persecutor of the church. Clearly, his deeply familiar Jewish audience offered no objection to what he said. Therefore, to suppose that *all* of the students of Shammai were violent rebels, while *all* of the students of Gamaliel were a bunch of peaceniks, reveals a strange presumption on Wright's part. Instead, we are much safer staying with the text, rather than venturing into the realm of the white spaces of Holy Writ.

In the end, Paul doesn't say when his decision for violent persecution came about. Perhaps it was that moment when he stood as a mere observer at the death of Stephen, or perhaps it was at another time. What we do know is that Paul came to his conclusion in such a manner that his mind had been changed by way of his own reason, and by this conviction of his he resolved to excel above others in his violent pursuit of the followers of Jesus Christ.

Paul, an Apostle of Jesus Christ

According to Wright, the confluence of Paul's past as a Shammaite Pharisee, along with his ministry as an Apostle of Christ, moved Paul to present a worldview that was "essentially Jewish...reworked around Jesus."[79] It is important to note that when Wright says "essentially Jewish" he is including the notion of a Pauline-Shammaite eschatology. However, his insistence on a Shammaite coloration in Paul's theology is nothing but a phantom that represents a direct contradiction to the Apostle's own words and actions. We should remember that Paul spoke

---

[79] Wright, Saint Paul, p. 79.

very reverently concerning his Apostleship in Christ Jesus. He also spoke very clearly of the newness of life that the believer has, over and above one's former manner of life. As a Christian, Paul was a *new creature in Christ (2 Cor. 5:17)*; he had been crucified with Christ and *it was no longer he who lived, but Christ lived in him (Gal. 2:20)*; what Paul was in Adam had been buried through baptism into death, so that he might walk in *newness of life (Romans 5-6)*. To suggest that Paul had any interest in borrowing from his *doubly dead past*, in order to serve the *living* Savior, is utterly ludicrous. It is here that we must say that for anyone to suppose that Paul's experience as a Pharisee had any significant impact on his teaching as an Apostle of Jesus Christ is quite unthinkable. Despite the labors of Wright to make Paul a Shammaite Pharisee, the discerning Christian must remember Paul's own valuation of his pharisaic upbringing:

Philippians 3:3-9: 3 "...for we are the true circumcision, who worship in the Spirit of God and glory in Christ Jesus and put no confidence in the flesh, 4 although I myself might have confidence even in the flesh. If anyone else has a mind to put confidence in the flesh, I far more: 5 circumcised the eighth day, of the nation of Israel, of the tribe of Benjamin, a Hebrew of Hebrews; as to the Law, a Pharisee; 6 as to zeal, a persecutor of the church; as to the righteousness which is in the Law, found blameless. 7 But whatever things were gain to me, those things I have counted as loss for the sake of Christ. 8 More than that, I count all things to be loss in view of the surpassing value of knowing Christ Jesus my Lord, for whom I have suffered the loss of all things, and count them but rubbish so that I may gain Christ, 9 and may be found in Him, not having a righteousness of my own derived from the Law, but that which is through faith in Christ, the righteousness which comes from God on the basis of faith..."

When Paul mentions his Jewish pedigree, to include his training in the law as a Pharisee, we must remember that everything that he revealed would have been prized by the Jewish community. No doubt, those of the "false circumcision" would have read with great admiration as they considered Paul's Jewish background; however this great mountain of Jewish achievement, delineated by Paul, was then given the real valuation it deserved: all of it was loss (G. *zēmian* v. 7), loss (G. *zēmian* v. 8) and rubbish (G. *skubala*, v. 8). It is as if Paul searched through the dregs of human language in order to describe the value of his past. All of his Jewish medals of honor were as *zēmian* (damaged goods) and *skubala*. That final word, *skubala*, literally means *dung*, making his great *mountain* of Jewish achievement a heap of human waste. Whatever traditionalism Paul had in his past as a Pharisee - it was that which no thinking human would go back to:

> *Philippians 3:13-14: 13 "...forgetting what lies behind and reaching forward to what lies ahead, 14 I press on toward the goal for the prize of the upward call of God in Christ Jesus."*

For Paul, reaching into his Christless past was nothing less than a disgusting idea. To suggest otherwise is to say that the Apostle would have gladly sorted through a dung heap for wisdom in his service to Christ. Paul was a new creature in Christ and therefore any dependence upon his dead past would have been like reaching into stench-filled crypt. Paul would find such teaching reprehensible. I would have to believe that if this Apostle of Christ were to meet anyone who argued against this point, he would offer nothing less than a stern rebuke reminding his critics that he was neither a Shammaite Pharisee, nor a follower of Gamaliel, - *instead Paul was an apostle of Jesus Christ – nothing more, nothing less.*

Indeed, Has Paul Really Said?

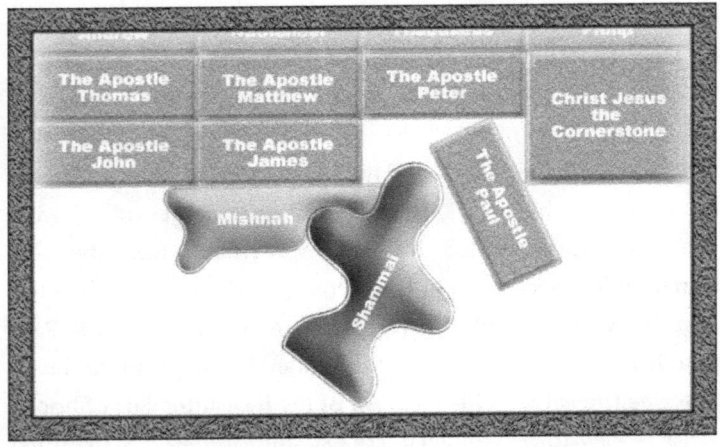

There is yet another matter to consider as we evaluate Wright's emphasis on a Pauline-Shammaite eschatology. It raises the question about Wright's own familiarity with historic Shammaite doctrine. Additionally, it makes one wonder if Wright understands the dangers that arise when one attempts to incorporate a phantom brick of Shammaite-Apostleship within the firm foundation of God's revelation. In his book *Everyman's Talmud*, Abraham Cohen offers the following description of the different views of Hillel and Shammai as they pertained to God's eschatological judgment of humanity. Anyone who is versed in the *Mishnah* will know that it frequently departs from the canon of the O.T., and thus advances what our Savior called *the traditions of men*. Since Wright wishes to infuse Shammaite thinking into Paul, it then behooves us to investigate what that eschatology entailed:

> "The locus classicus on the subject [of God's eschatological judgment] reads: 'The School of Shammai declared, *There will be three groups on the Day of Judgment: one of thoroughly righteous people, one of thoroughly wicked people and one of people in between.*

The first group will be immediately inscribed for everlasting life; the second group will be doomed in Gehinnom, as it says, 'And many of them that sleep in the dust of the earth shall awake, some to everlasting life and some to reproaches and everlasting abhorrence' [Daniel 12:2], the third will go down to Gehinnom and squeal and rise again, as it says, "And I will bring the third part through the fire, and will refine them as silver is refined, and will try them as gold is tried. They shall call on My name and I will answer them."[80]

The school of Shammai taught that in the final judgment, there will be three classes of humanity: *1. the thoroughly righteous, 2. the thoroughly wicked and 3. those who are "in between."* By these categories it is evident that the school of Shammai taught:

1. Moral perfectionism by the law [perfectly righteous],

2. Moral depravity [those doomed to Gehinnom].

3. Moral neutrality [those who are in between the righteous and the wicked].

In view of this, a critical question arises: if we are to believe that Paul's theology was somehow informed by a Shammaite tradition, then what would prevent the reader from assuming that Paul embraced the peculiar idea of moral neutrality or even a form of purgatory ["the third will go down to Gehinnom and squeal and rise again..."]? By this teaching it is evident that the Shammaites believed that men could atone for their own sins through suffering – a very common belief held within the oral traditions of the Pharisees:

---

[80] Abraham Cohen, Everyman's Talmud, pp. 377-78 [See also the Babylonian Talmud, tractate Rosh Hashanah 16b-17a].

> *"'There are chastenings which purge all the iniquities of man' (Ber. 5a); 'Whoever manifests the symptoms of plague is to regard them as nothing but an altar of atonement' (ibid. 5b); 'Let a man rejoice in sufferings more than in happiness; for if a man has lived all his life in happiness, any sin which he may have committed has not been pardoned; but what is pardoned through suffering is forgiven him...'Three classes of persons will not behold the face of Gehinnom: they who have suffered the afflictions of poverty, disease of the bowels, and the tyranny of Roman rule' (Erub. 4Ib)."*[81]

It is this very concept of *atonement through suffering* that is reflected in the disciples' naïve question in John 9 – *"Rabbi, who sinned, this man or his parents, that he should be born blind?"* But Christ was clearly not influenced by such oral traditions:

> John 9:3: 3 Jesus answered, "It was neither that this man sinned, nor his parents; but it was so that the works of God might be displayed in him."

Clearly, the first century landscape was saturated with *Pharisaical traditions*, and yet it was Christ who faithfully rebuked them, calling them the very means by which God's Word was transgressed.[82] No matter what doctrinal subject we may consult, it is essential to remember that the Christian's hope is not found in the extra-biblical writings of any scribe or Pharisee.

Finally, our aforementioned Shammaite eschatology reveals another false view of human nature: If men can be thoroughly righteous by their own works, then man's depravity is not *total*.

---

[81] Ibid., p. 106.
[82] Matthew 15:1-14.

Paul's Apostleship

This reveals what is brazenly obvious: most Pharisaic traditions were couched in a kind of works-righteousness scheme which stands as a precursor to semi-pelagianism throughout history. In view of this, those who wish to argue that Paul was influenced by a Shammaite theology are playing with a strange and dangerous fire. The firm foundation upon which Paul stood had nothing to do with the extra-biblical traditions of men.[83] Instead, Paul's message was calibrated by only one cornerstone – Jesus Christ Himself.

For Wright, justification is not about how a person is saved by means of Christ's righteousness - it is an eschatological concept that looks to the confirmation that believers are already members of God's kingdom - a fact that will be fully revealed in the final judgment. This idea is then believed to replace the historic concept of *justification by the imputation of Christ's righteousness.* In order to get to this conclusion Mr. Wright had to be willing to do violence to the biblical record itself through an exaltation of extra-biblical "authorities." It is here that Martin Luther's rebuke of Erasmus comes to mind, and I will now apply it to Mr. Wright:

> *"It is hard to put it down to ignorance on your part, for you are no longer young, you have lived among Christians, and you have long studied the sacred writings; you leave me no room to make excuses for you or to think well of you."*[84]

Like Erasmus, Mr. Wright has not a lack of education or experience in life to excuse these injustices to the doctrine of justification by faith, and the masses who are being led astray by

---

[83] Ephesians 2:20 having been built upon the foundation of the apostles and prophets, Christ Jesus Himself being the corner stone,

[84] Luther, Bondage of the Will, p. 74.

this man are being escorted away from the Scriptures in the name of modern scholasticism. It is an extremely sad *and dangerous* ordeal in the modern day. By incorporating Shammai into the teaching of the Apostle, we resultantly corrupt the teachings of the Scriptures themselves.

Chapter 4

The Righteousness of God and The Whole Counsel of God

In this final chapter we will take a step back and consider the broader implications of what we have studied thus far concerning the righteousness of God. As you'll recall from chapter one, our examination of the ancient Hebrew word *ṣedeq* led us to consider the threefold categories of thought concerning the ethical, forensic, and theocratic aspects of God's righteousness. This semantic domain established a crucial foundation of thought concerning the Greek word *dikaios*, as well as the expression *dikaiosunē theou* - the righteousness of God. In all of this we find that these categories of thought are still sustained within the New Testament, however with *multiple Christ-centered realities.* In other words, the Old Testament's presentation of God's righteousness is ultimately a foreshadowing of what would be revealed in the person of the Lord Jesus Christ:

Jeremiah 23:5-6 5 "Behold, the days are coming," declares the Lord, "When I shall raise up for David a righteous Branch; And He will reign as king and act wisely And do justice and righteousness in the land. 6 "In His days Judah will be saved, and Israel will dwell securely; And this is His name by which He will be called, 'The Lord our righteousness.'"

Clearly, the righteous Branch of David, who is also called *The Lord our righeousness* [yhwh ṣidqenû (from > ṣedeq)], is in fact the Lord Jesus Christ. Jeremiah 23:6 reminds us that the multifaceted contributions of every biblical writer points to a unified and harmonious message concerning God's righteous nature and works. Additionally, we cannot forget that even though the biblical writers were themselves *mutable men,* they were miraculously used of God to deliver an immutable message. Thus, while we can always detect certain nuances between the human instruments of Scripture, there are still no such nuances that would ever render a contradiction between them – *God is not the author of confusion*.[85] Jeremiah 23:6 also reminds us that if every single word, *iōta*, and *keraia* of Scripture must be treated with great regard,[86] then the name of God Himself (*yhwh ṣidqenû*) must never be handled with any less care than the rest. It is for this reason that I have warned the reader about the dangers that come with any redaction of such terms and concepts. Even the slightest modification of any such term or concept can create an upheaval of truth in the rest of Scripture – even the very name of God. Imagine if a quantum physicist could tweak the force of gravity (even just a little bit), he would be doing more than just modifying a single force in nature – *he would end up transforming the entire universe itself.* And so it is with Paul and his teachings. Since the 66 books of the Bible are so indelibly linked together in a harmony that can only be attributed to One Author, the Lord God Himself, then every student of Scripture must understand that it is a dangerous matter to trifle with any aspect of Holy Writ. After all, it is not *ours* with which to trifle at all.

Jesus Christ the Righteous

A careful study of God's Word reveals that the writers of Scripture passed along a unified and meaningful revelation of the Lord Jesus Christ, thus demonstrating that they were harmoniously carried along by the Holy Spirit. In fact, this is

---

[85] 1 Corinthians 14:33.
[86] Matthew 5:18.

what the Savior promised that the Holy Spirit would do after the Lord Himself ascended to be with the Father:

> John 16:8-11: 8 "And He, when He comes, will convict the world concerning sin, and righteousness, and judgment; 9 concerning sin, because they do not believe in Me; 10 and concerning righteousness, because I go to the Father, and you no longer behold Me; 11 and concerning judgment, because the ruler of this world has been judged."

Christ's departure from the world would in no way eradicate the revelation of God's righteousness among men. It is this very promise, given to Christ's Apostles, that was also entrusted to the Apostle Paul such that through their Apostolic labors and writings, the Holy Spirit would reveal God's righteousness to this fallen world. Texts such as these ought to strengthen our expectations of finding a harmonious message among the New Testament writers concerning the righteousness of God as revealed in the person of Jesus Christ. In this final chapter, we will test that expectation by consulting one writer who also said a great deal about God's righteousness, and that is the Apostle John. In particular, we will examine John's first epistle where he employs the term *dikaios* no less than eleven times as a positive expression of God's righteousness, and as an antithetical expression denoting mankind's unrighteousness.

If John's epistle is anything, it is a New Covenant study on the nature and power of God's own righteousness versus the unrighteousness of this world order. In many respects his treatment of the *righteousness of God* corresponds to our prior lexical examination of *ṣedeq/dikaios* in chapter one. All in all, the Apostle John yields for us the evidences of the ethical, forensic, and theocratic realities of God's righteousness throughout his letter, with Christ as the centerpiece of it all:

Ethical Righteousness and the Christian: The Christian's obedience to God's commandments is a repeated theme for John. This is why his epistle is seen as providing several tests for valid faith in the life of a believer: *1 John 2:3-4; 3 And by this we know that we have come to know Him, if we keep His commandments. 4 The one who says, "I have come to know Him," and does not keep His commandments, is a liar, and the truth is not in him;"* Therefore John lets us know that this world yields a very clear polarity *as evidenced* by the presence of God's ethical righteousness in the life of a believer, or the absence thereof in the life of the unbeliever: *1 John 3:10: "By this the children of God and the children of the devil are obvious: anyone who does not practice righteousness is not of God, nor the one who does not love his brother."*

Theocratic Righteousness/Faithfulness and the Christian: In addition to John's emphasis on God's righteousness is this concept of Christ's victory as the source of blessing for His people (John 16:33, Rev. 5:5 & 1 John 5:4). Thus, the triumph of God's righteous kingdom is evidenced in the life of His children at three distinct levels: *salvation (1 John 5:1-4), sanctification (1 John 2:29), and future glorification (1 John 3:1-3).* In all of this we see that God is faithful in displaying His righteousness in and through His church here on the earth by redeeming us in the righteousness His Son, sanctifying us in the righteousness of His Son, and glorifying us in the righteousness His Son.

These categories of thought (*theocratic and ethical righteousness*) clearly dominate John's epistle, and they comport with his simple conclusion at the end when he writes: "Little Children, guard yourselves from idols." As the children of God, and as the members of His righteous kingdom, believers are to practice God's righteousness rather than embrace the idolatry of this defeated world. God in Christ is displaying His faithful victory amidst His people, and it is our responsibility and privilege to convey that victory through lives that are being brought into conformity with God's own righteousness.

But what does John have to say, if anything, about God's *forensic righteousness? Plenty*. Not only does John speak to this important issue, but it establishes the necessary premise for all that he has to say in the rest of his epistle. In fact, should we fail to comprehend what John reveals concerning God's forensic righteousness *then we would end up missing his entire message concerning the person and work of Jesus Christ.* John's description of forensic righteousness in 1 John 2:1-2 establishes the necessary doctrine concerning the child of God's *position* in Christ as a necessary prelude to the description of our *practice* and *victory* in Christ. Failure to establish this grammatical premise of John's can only lead to gross misunderstandings concerning the remainder of his epistle because of this simple truth: *Men are not made the sons of God because of their servitude; rather, men serve because they are the sons of God - in Christ.* John's point is quite clear throughout his letter: *what is antecedent to a Christian's obedience is their forgiveness of sin and regeneration through the Holy Spirit.* In other words, without regeneration (1 John 2:29, 3:9, 4:7, 5:1, 4) and the mercy of forgiveness in the life of God's elect (2:1-2), there would be no redemptive manifestation of God's ethical and theocratic righteousness in this world whatsoever. Ultimately, forensic righteousness supplies the bedrock foundation upon which all other manifestations of God's righteousness do depend:

1 John 2:1-2: 1 My little children, I am writing these things to you that you may not sin. And if anyone sins, we have an Advocate with the Father, Jesus Christ the righteous; 2 and He Himself is the propitiation for our sins; and not for ours only, but also for those of the whole world.

One of the great disasters that I have seen take place concerning the handling of 1 John is when expositors fail to recognize the foundational nature of John's premise to his entire argument. And what is his premise? His premise is centered on a person who is called by name: *The Word of Life (1 John 1:1), who is, Jesus Christ the Righteous (1 John 2:1)*. The remainder of the epistle is a further description of what a Christian's *new life* and *righteous conduct* should look like as patterned after the One who is the very source of all life and righteousness. John's emphasis on God's forensic righteousness is clearly revealed when he mentions "Jesus Christ the righteous" as the central identity of the One who is our: *1. Advocate with the Father and 2. Propitiation for our sins.* Grammatically speaking, Christ's name (Jesus Christ the righteous) identifies with each office – *Advocate and propitiation,* and therefore we must remember that John is identifying the Savior as our *righteous* Advocate and as our *righteous* propitiation:

Our Righteous Advocate

The NASB translation uses the word *Advocate* to represent the Greek word *parcklēton*. It is this same term that is used by Christ for the Holy Spirit: *John 14:16 "...I will ask the Father, and He will give you another Helper, that He may be with you forever;"* Clearly the Holy Spirit is called *another* Helper (*allon paraklēton*) because it is *Jesus Christ the righteous* who is the believer's principal Advocate within the judiciary of God. I mention the word judiciary here because the word *paraklēton* is an unmistakable reference to that of a legal advisor or advocate in a court of law.[87] Rabbinic scholars employed this term to refer to the *advocacy* of sin offerings before God,[88] and it was even used in reference to one's own good works in the same vein of a Shammaite soteriology:

> "All the benevolences and good works which the Israelites do in this world ... are great advocates [*prqlytwn - paracletes*] between the Israelites and their Father in heaven" *Baba Batra 10a*.

The contrast between the pharisaic and biblical use of this word is quite profound: John is clearly teaching us that there is only One who can stand in the tribunal of God as our Advocate due to His *perfect righteousness* — it is Jesus Christ the righteous. Thus, Richard Rothe and Charles Haddon Spurgeon are right when they say, respectively:

> "Only the righteous One, the guiltless, the One that is separate from sin, can be the Advocate with God for sinners, in general the Mediator of salvation, and make His friendship for us prevalent with God, because only such a One has access to God and fellowship with God."[89]

---

[87] "...the history of the term in the whole sphere of known Greek and Hellenistic usage outside the NT yields the clear picture of a legal adviser or helper or advocate in the relevant court." Kittel, TDNT, Vol. 5, p. 802.

[88] "The sin offering is like the *prqlyt* (paraclete) which comes forward to appease (the judge)." Rabbi Shimon, Sifra Leviticus 277a on Leviticus 14:19.

[89] Richard Rothe in The Expositor's Greek Testament, ed. W. Robertson Nicoll (WM B. Eerdmans Publishing Company, Grand Rapids MI), Vol. 5, p. 172.

"'Jesus Christ the righteous.' This is not only his character but his plea. It is his character, and if the Righteous One be my advocate, then my cause is good, or he would not have espoused it. It is his plea, for he meets the charge of unrighteousness against me by the plea that he is righteous. He declares himself my substitute and puts his obedience to my account. My soul, thou hast a friend well fitted to be thine advocate, he cannot but succeed; leave thyself entirely in his hands."[90]

What John presents to us in 1 John 2:1 is no *cold piece of business.* Instead, he entrusts to us a blessed and heart-warming portrait of our Lord and Savior whose once-for-all blood-sacrifice *mercifully pleads* our case within the judiciary of God. Remove Jesus Christ the righteous from this scene, and we are left with nothing but the just judgment of God Himself. His advocacy is therefore the *foundational reason* why the believer can stand in confidence when He appears (1 John 2:28), and this very message of the Holy Spirit, through the Apostle John, is given to us as well through the Apostle Paul who spoke of Christ's advocacy in these terms:

"Therefore, having been justified by faith we now have peace with God through our Lord Jesus Christ" (Romans 5:1).

This precious portrait of our Savior, standing on our behalf as our righteous Advocate, is the unified message of John, Paul, and every other Spirit-led writer of the Scriptures.

---

[90] Spurgeon, C. H. Morning and Evening: Daily readings (October 4 PM). Oak Harbor, WA: Logos Research Systems, Inc.

Indeed, Has Paul Really Said?

Our Righteous Propitiation

John continues his teaching in 1 John 2:2 stating that "...He Himself is the propitiation for our sins." The grammar of John's declaration is quite clear - the objective identity of Christ in verse one is claimed as the subject in verse two such that we have this clear truth: *"He Himself (Jesus Christ the righteous)...is the propitiation for our sins."* John's use of the intensive pronoun/linking verb construction, *autos estin hilasmós* [Lit. Himself, He is propitiation] shows that John wants to identify *Jesus Christ the righteous* as the sole source of propitiation for our sin. His emphasis, along with the definition of propitiation is crucial: John is establishing the crucial truth that only Christ, and His righteousness *alone,* can supply the sacrificial satisfaction for God's justice. The term *hilasmós* speaks of a sacrifice that is offered to satisfy God's justice in view of sin. Conceptually, this is what Paul alludes to when he speaks of Christ's substitutionary sacrifice on our behalf:

> Galatians 3:13 Christ redeemed us from the curse of the Law, having become a curse for us—for it is written, "Cursed is everyone who hangs on a tree."

The gifts of redemption, mercy, and forgiveness are granted to the sinner on the basis of Christ's sacrifice on their behalf, whereby *He became a curse for us.* It is this very concept of Christ's propitiation that is central to His ministry as our High Priest:

> Hebrews 2:17 Therefore, He had to be made like His brethren in all things, that He might become a merciful and faithful high priest in

things pertaining to God, to make propitiation for the sins of the people.

But if it were not for the purity and perfection of Christ's righteousness, His sacrifice could in no way appease the *immutably-righteous* justice of the Father. The supremacy of Christ's righteousness is even heralded in the order of His priesthood, which is of the order of Melchizedek (H. *mălkiy-ṣedeq – king of righteousness*). It is in this priestly order that Christ was declared[91] to be a priest forever.[92] We must not loose the important proclamation concerning *the righteousness of God* in the person and work of *Jesus Christ the righteous* – He is our *righteous* Advocate, and our *righteous* propitiation. Our sins were credited to Him, so that His righteousness would be credited to us - so that we now stand in God's judiciary as His beloved children *in Christ*. What John teaches us in 1 John 2:1-2 is the very same message given to us by the Apostle Paul in 2 Corinthians 5:21. It is the very language of exchange and substitution. It is the language of forgiveness, redemption, and genuine Christian joy; and it is the harmonious language of the *other Paraclete*, the Holy Spirit, who came to testify concerning the righteousness of God in Christ.

In all of this we see that John relates to us the full orb of truth concerning the righteousness of God, from the forensic to the theocratic, and ethical manifestations. As joined together, it is a harmonious message, not just *from* the Apostle John himself, but also *alongside* the Apostle Paul. God is not the author of

---

[91] Psalm 110.
[92] Hebrews 7:1-22.

confusion, and His messengers have spoken with one clear voice concerning Jesus Christ the righteous.

Sola Scriptura

In light of these things, I must say that it is quite sad, even alarming, that a man like Mr. Wright, who has such a reputation for being a devoted scholar of the Apostle Paul, should belie that reputation through such a limited and twisted presentation of the Scriptures themselves. Throughout history men have always wielded religious control over the masses by either withholding the Scriptures, or by offering secretive and obscure interpretations of Sacred Writ. With Roman Catholicism this was accomplished by withholding Bibles from the laity while mystifying their services with Latin. As well, we can credit ancient Gnosticism, along with the innovative theologies of modern liberalism, for the heaps of obscurity that have effectively kept myriads of people from the truth of God. All of this amounts to a religious control of the people, much like that of the Pharisees, whose oral traditions, myths, superstitions, and obfuscations of Scripture led not to a clarification of God's revelation, but to a nullification of it.[93] As a pastor, I have a great dread in my soul for what awaits the future of the church in America. Should the influence of such innovative teachings gain ground, then the true church of Jesus Christ will face an even greater challenge. My concern is not an insipid one, but it is grave in view of the magnitude of Wright's errors. Thus, I am not concerned that the doctrine of justification will *merely fail to flourish where N.T. Wright's*

---

[93] Matthew 15:1-9.

portrayal holds sway, rather, I fear that it utterly dies in such barren territory. We need a new reformation, but without the clear and unpolluted message of God's Word, such a reformation can never come about. I would even suggest that instead of seeking a *new and innovative perspective on Paul*, that we should seek out the *old and ancient perspective* that he gave concerning the sufficiency of all of Scripture, as delivered by all the biblical writers. This is the old Paul that we read about, who reminded Timothy about the sufficiency of the ancient and sacred Scriptures – *"All Scripture is inspired by God and profitable for teaching, for reproof, for correction, for training in righteousness."*[94] Paul's emphasis on *all Scripture* is a crucial one, for without the *unified* counsel of God's Word, Paul knew that he would not be able to minister to Christ's sheep:

> *Acts 20:24-27: 24 "But none of these things move me; nor do I count my life dear to myself, so that I may finish my race with joy, and the ministry which I received from the Lord Jesus, to testify to the gospel of the grace of God. 25 "And indeed, now I know that you all, among whom I have gone preaching the kingdom of God, will see my face no more. 26 "Therefore I testify to you this day that I am innocent of the blood of all men. 27 "For I have not shunned to declare to you the whole counsel of God."*

The only reason why Paul had a clear conscience before God and men is that he lived a life that was dedicated to the unified revelation given by the Holy Spirit; that is, the message of *the whole counsel of God as revealed in the God-breathed Scriptures.*

---

[94] 2 Timothy 3:16.

Indeed, Has Paul Really Said?

Paul's Wisdom is our Warning

It is here that we must remember that adjusting the meaning of single word or phrase can yield devastating effects on one's theology. As well, by isolating a single author of Scripture and foisting artificial contexts and connotations onto his writings, we can resultantly malign the harmonious message of God's Word. As Paul taught very clearly, the foundation of God's Word is established by the surety and perfection of Jesus Christ Himself:

> Ephesians 2:19-20: So then you are no longer strangers and aliens, but you are fellow citizens with the saints, and are of God's household, 20 having been built upon the foundation of the apostles and prophets, Christ Jesus Himself being the corner stone...

It is certainly not the point of this chapter to deny the individuality and uniqueness of the human authors of Scripture. However, the presence of human individuality does not supplant the overall authorship of the Holy Spirit,[95] nor does it nullify the unity of His message. Because of this, I would submit to the reader that it is quite troubling whenever a theologian advances a system of thought that puts the writers of Holy Writ in a state of contradiction with one another.

---

[95] 2 Peter 1:20-21.

The Whole Counsel of God

Summary

For several years now, I have seen the subtleties of liberal influences upon modern exegesis. A number of years ago I attended a pastor's conference for the Evangelical Free association in Forest Falls California. In one particular session I was treated to an afternoon of teaching which consisted of the "Psychology of Jonah" - a series of lessons which sought to reveal Jonah's thoughts and feelings as he was fleeing his God-ordained responsibilities. Questions like - *"What do you think was going through Jonah's mind when he did these things?"* and *"how do you think he felt when he was swallowed by that big fish?"* constituted the inductive drivel of the day. For myself, it was an opportunity to remember, among many other things, my great privilege to serve God's people as a teacher of Holy Writ - and nothing else.

At the end of this event I had realized that the "teacher" had said precious little regarding Jonah's sin, his rebellion; nor was there even a whisper given concerning the mercy and absolute sovereignty of God in everything. I count that event as just another opportunity for me to witness, firsthand, the destructive effects of liberalism in the church because it is often the case that whatever isn't explicitly revealed in the Scriptures often becomes *le plat principal*, while that which is revealed in Holy Writ is sadly treated as unwanted scraps. Thus, there is a great danger that comes when men believe that their extrabiblical speculation has sufficient warrant to supplant biblical revelation. It is this same danger that is rising up within modern Evangelicalism, and men like N.T. Wright are fostering such an emergence. However, without *Holy Writ* we are rudderless ships, drifting through an endless sea of human speculation. Additionally, the Bible doesn't *need* our creative thinking, innovative speculations, nor does it depend upon our ability to know every personal nuance of the writers of Holy Writ in order for us to understand and submit to its authoritative message. Simply put - Scripture is profitable *because* it is inspired *by God (as Paul taught)* - not by you; not by me; not by any other living pastor/preacher/teacher or author - God alone. Scripture is sufficient apart from any contributions by men (no matter how educated they are). Whenever we modify what God has revealed, we end up adding nothing but that which is worthy of judgment. Holy Writ must remain unmolested by the hands of men, and as Christians we must resist that distrustful query delivered by the serpent: *"Indeed, has God really said?"* Perhaps the greatest dangers to the church come not in the form of the *explicit denials* of Scripture, but in the gradual expressions of *doubt, distrust and liberal perplexity.*

Wright's treatment of extra-biblical history, and Scripture itself, does call into question his understanding of the relative authority of each. Clearly, the historical-grammatical method relies on a measure of extra-biblical history, and yet, it must always be remembered that *biblical history will always trump extra-biblical history* for the simple reason that God's Word is always superior to any written record of man. That simple truth, if applied correctly, would single-handedly refute the overwhelming majority of Wright's arguments and conclusions in his book. It is for this reason that I question Mr. Wright's understanding of the supremacy of Scriptural authority in light of his many omissions, infusions, and his overall modern use of the Bible:

1. Wright's Omissions: *As we have already discussed, Wright avoids a great deal of Scripture when revealing his view of the Jewish courtroom. However, the amount of Scriptural references that are dedicated to God's judiciary is quite robust, and yet Wright manages to avoid nearly all of it, especially references employed by Christ and the Apostle Paul. As well, Paul's clear argument regarding his tutelage at the feet of Gamaliel is yet another truth that is entirely bypassed by Wright. It is as though Paul's own words about his life are entirely dismissible because of Wright's argument. By arguing that Paul's theology was colored by his pharisaical past, Wright is later forced to make some conflicting conclusions about Paul's doctrinal convictions: "If later, as a Christian, he argues for positions (on divorce, for instance) which are more like those of the Hillelites, that must be seen as part of the effect of his conversion, not as reflecting the agendas he had embraced in his pre-Christian state."[96] Statements like these reveal Wright's own logical self-entrapment. His presumptions of pharisaical influences in Paul force him to yield such "tricks of thought." However, if we stick with what Paul really did say, then we must conclude that he was an Apostle of Jesus Christ, and as such, Paul had no other Rabbi at whose feet he sat and learned, or from which he taught than that of Jesus Christ.*

2. Wright's Infusions: *Wright's appetite for extra-biblical authority should be unsettling to any student of Scripture. I should say here that any exegete must examine 1st century history if he expects to understand the contemporary context of the biblical writers; and yet, extra-biblical history must be handled with great care, understanding that it is not equal with Scripture and is subject to flaws and faulty interpretation. A great variety of contemporary extra-biblical resources ought to be consulted when considering 1st century history*

---

[96] Wright, Saint Paul, p. 30.

- but this must be done with the understanding that biblical history must always trump extra-biblical history. Reverse the order of these things, and you'll supplant God's authority everywhere.

3. Wright's Modern Use of the Bible: *At the ending of his book we find, perhaps, the most confounding discovery in the whole book. There we find, as mentioned at the beginning, that Mr. Wright's ultimate agenda is that of a new and modern ecumenism, as cited earlier: "It cannot be right that the very doctrine which declares that all who believe in Jesus belong at the same table (Galatians 2) should be used as a way of saying that some, who define the doctrine of justification differently, belong at a different table. The doctrine of justification, in other words, is not merely a doctrine which Catholic and Protestant might just be able to agree on, as a result of hard ecumenical endeavor. It is itself the ecumenical doctrine, the doctrine that rebukes all our petty and often culture-bound church groupings, and which declares that all who believe in Jesus belong together in the one family."[97] And should the reader doubt Wright's conviction on this need for ecumenism, we find him making this statement a few pages later: "Any attempt to define church membership by anything other than allegiance to Jesus Christ is, quite simply, idolatrous."[98] It is at this point that the reader must realize that all of Wright's biblical omissions and infusions have served this central purpose - to establish an ecumenism which embraces Roman Catholicism and Protestantism at the same time.*

As to this last point, even Rome knows better than this. The historic divide between a *works-righteousness synergism* and a *justification-by-faith monergism* is the difference between night and day; and if the Bible can't bridge that divide, then any bridge crafted by men is a mere sham.

---

[97] Ibid., p. 158.
[98] Ibid., p. 160.

There is also a question that remains about Wright's view of the afterlife. In this and other works, Wright has not been very forthright about his own views of heaven and hell. As one of his conclusions to *What Saint Paul Really Said* Wright discloses the following:

> "...the covenant between God and Israel was always designed to be God's means of saving the whole world. It was never supposed to be the means whereby God would have a private little group of people who would be saved while the rest of the world went to hell (whatever you might mean by that). Thus, when God is faithful to the covenant in the death and resurrection of Jesus Christ and in the work of the Spirit, it makes nonsense of the Pauline gospel to imagine that the be-all and end-all of this operation is so that God can have another, merely different, private little group of people who are saved while the world is consigned to the cosmic waste-paper basket."[99]

It is here that I must ask: *Does Mr. Wright believe in a literal hell; that is, a place of eternal torment for the lost? If he does believe in hell, is he denying that God will someday condemn men to eternal judgment? - or as he says - "[a] world consigned to the cosmic waste-paper basket."* It is in this very statement that I would ask: "Is Wright influenced by a Shammaite eschatology himself?" As you'll recall:

> "'The School of Shammai declared, There will be three groups on the Day of Judgment: one of thoroughly righteous people, one of thoroughly wicked people and one of people in between. The first group will be immediately inscribed for everlasting life; the second group will be doomed in Gehinnom], as it says, 'And many of them that sleep in the dust of the earth shall awake, some to everlasting life and some to reproaches and everlasting abhorrence' [Daniel 12:2],

---

[99] Ibid., p. 163.

the third will go down to Gehinnom and squeal and rise again, *as it says, "And I will bring the third part through the fire, and will refine them as silver is refined, and will try them as gold is tried. They shall call on My name and I will answer them"*[100]

As mentioned earlier, there is within the thinking of the Shammaite Pharisee a kind of second chance for those who are *morally neutral* - a second chance for the *not so wicked and not so righteous who will be able to atone for their own sins by their suffering.* This smacks of the Roman Catholic doctrine of purgatory and seems to coincide with his call for ecumenism. It is at this point that I can anticipate the protests coming right away. There are many zealous defenders of Wright who would strongly protest the notion that anyone should dare to question the man's commitment to Holy Writ, but Wright's treatment of the Bible is in fact troubling for anyone who cares to observe the facts at hand. We often hear of Wright's noble defenses of the doctrine of the resurrection – I am sure that they are quite good; and yet we must also remember that the Pharisees were the champions of the doctrine of the resurrection in their day – but this in no way made them friends of the Gospel. It is much like the many experiences that I have had in visiting churches. Many churches will herald the doctrine of inerrancy in their doctrinal statements, and yet there are many of these same churches that fall short of *applying and preaching core church doctrines:* the gospel itself, church discipline, or the biblical roles of men and women. To say that the Bible is authoritative is one thing, but how one treats the Bible becomes the real moment of truth.

---

[100] Cohen, Everyman's Talmud, pp. 377-78.

I must submit to the reader that Wright's treatment of Holy Writ is quite concerning. In many respects the Bible has become a mere tool for him to advance an agenda of ecumenism - and those who oppose what he says are then guilty of idolatry, or as he says, *"any attempt to define church membership by anything other than allegiance to Jesus Christ is, quite simply, idolatrous."* While that statement may seem agreeable to the casual reader, the question must then be asked - *which Jesus?* The Jesus of Rome? The Jesus of modern liberalism? The Jesus of Paul, the "Shammaite Pharisee"?

I can at least agree with Mr. Wright that allegiance to Jesus Christ alone is essential if we are to avoid the sin of idolatry, but in order to pursue *Jesus alone, we must know Him by the Scriptures alone.* No omissions, no infusions, and no innovations: Just Christ *alone*, by grace *alone*, through faith in Him *alone*, through the Scriptures *alone* - all for the glory of God *alone*.

Conclusion

A Tale of Two Contests

Indeed, Has Paul Really Said?

We will now conclude our journey together with a *tale of two contests* which will help us to summarize our study of *the righteousness of God*. To begin with let me say that in God's good providence, my earlier mention the schools of Shammai and Hillel will supply us with our first tale. As you may have surmised already, both the schools of Shammai and Hillel were often found to be at odds with each other. In some sense, we can think of their opposing theologies as if they were overlapping waves – oscillating from one extreme to another, while only occasionally intersecting the axis itself, that is to say, the axis of God's Word. The more these schools were plagued with the oral traditions of men, the more they oscillated and strayed from such an axis of God's truth. The Talmud tells the story of one such period of competing oscillations between these two schools. It had to do with a lengthy contest over the question concerning the sinfulness of man: *In view of mankind's sinfulness, should he have ever been created in the first place?* The school of Hillel asserted the following answer:

> "It were better if man had not been created; but inasmuch as he has been created, let him examine his works." - (Hillel School. Talmud: Erubim 13b)

According to the tradition,[101] this contest lasted for two and a half years, after which time a count was taken and the majority accepted the conclusion of Hillel (*it would have been better that*

---

[101] "The Talmud records that 'two and a half years the School of Shammai and the School of Hillel were divided on the following point: The latter maintained that it had been better if man had never been created. The count was taken and the majority decided that it would have been better if he had not been created; but since he has been created, let him investigate his (past) actions. Another version is: Let him examine his (present) actions." Cohen, Everyman's Talmud, p. 95.

man had never been created). For the school of Hillel it was seen as a great victory, but in reality *no one from either school won*. If there is a victor at all emerging from the background of this story, his name is Paul of Tarsus whose own answer pierced through the capricious oscillations of all human reason. Most importantly, Paul's answer was as straight as an arrow for the simple reason that *he was an Apostle of Jesus Christ who spoke by the inspiration of the Holy Spirit*. When Paul answered this question, he did not utilize the man-centered reasoning of Shammai or Hillel. He did not begin with Hillel's emphasis on mankind's sinfulness and corruption; nor did he borrow from Shammai's emphasis on mankind's value and supposed ability to be *perfectly righteous*. Instead, his answer began and ended with a vision of the ultimate glory of the *righteous* Potter:

> Romans 9:21-24: 21 ...does not the potter have a right over the clay, to make from the same lump one vessel for honorable use, and another for common use? 22 What if God, although willing to demonstrate His wrath and to make His power known, endured with much patience vessels of wrath prepared for destruction? 23 And He did so in order that He might make known the riches of His glory upon vessels of mercy, which He prepared beforehand for glory, 24 even us, whom He also called, not from among Jews only, but also from among Gentiles.

As an Apostle of Jesus Christ, Paul had no more use for the man-centered theology of his past training. As a child of God he understood that the real question isn't – *Should man ever have been made, but instead: will God be glorified through His righteous display of wrath and redemption?* The answer to this latter question is, of course, a resounding *yes!* Paul's mention of God's display of wrath and redemption should sound familiar to you. This is the same summary offered as the pretext of Paul's argument, where in Romans 1:17-18 he spoke of God's work of *displaying His righteousness*, through *justification (v. 17)* and through His *just judgment (v. 18)*. If it seems that Paul keeps hitting the same nail on the head, he is. The stubborn and wooden theologies of men require such repetition, for the supremacy and sovereignty of God is clearly not the product of human thinking or logic. Thus, having had a lifetime of experience with those who reasoned by such human wisdom,[102] Paul anticipated all naysayers by reminding them of the Potter's *righteous sovereignty over the clay:*

> Romans 9:14-16: 14 What shall we say then? There is no injustice with God, is there? May it never be! 15 For He says to Moses, "I will have mercy on whom I have mercy, and I will have compassion on whom I have compassion." 16 So then it does not depend on the man who wills or the man who runs, but on God who has mercy.

Is there *injustice (adikía)* in God? *May it never be!* As you will recall, this is the very same inquiry made by Paul in Romans 3:5:

> Romans 3:5 But if our unrighteousness demonstrates the righteousness of God, what shall we say? The God who inflicts wrath is not unrighteous, is He? (I am speaking in human terms.)

Paul spent a great deal of time answering this very question – "Is God unrighteous?" This really boils down to the query about what is *right* or *fair*. By mankind's crooked standard of righteousness – it doesn't seem *right* that the Potter should be sovereign over the clay. The sinful human heart wants to cry

---

[102] Romans 9:14,19: 14 What shall we say then? There is no injustice with God, is there? May it never be! 19 You will say to me then, "Why does He still find fault? For who resists His will?"

out, *"this is unjust!"* But by the reality of God's eternal and immutable righteousness *there is no injustice in God, and there never will be.* By this, that ancient contest between the schools of Hillel and Shammai withers away into insignificance beneath the towering reality of the Potter's *righteous* sovereignty, wrath, mercy, and eternal glory.

End of contest #1.

And where is the tale of our second contest? Well the details of that story are still being worked out. In the present day, there are various schools of novelty that often contest with one another over various matters of doctrine, however, a more modern school has advanced this query about *what Saint Paul really said.* It is this very school which champions a *New Perspective on Paul,* and they are seeking to obtain a majority count within the realm of professing Christendom. Whether they will ever gain the majority view or not has yet to be seen, but I can say that no matter what may happen in the future, the authorities of this school have already lost the contest from the very beginning. The basis of their position is plainly a false one, for the premise of their research is far too man-centered. Frankly speaking, their theological perspective is focused on a single man – Paul of Tarsus – *and an invented version of him at that.* However, God's truth cannot be altered by the creative redactions of scholars who might posit a new perspective on any human author of Holy Writ, because the ultimate author of all Scripture is the Lord God Himself. By focusing too much on this one human instrument of God's revelation, the *School of NPP* has resultantly substituted the Christian's basis of authority from *Thus saith the Lord* to *thus saith the gatekeepers of NPP.* What we have yet to discover in this contest is whether or not this will be another passing fancy and designer theology, casually embraced by the shallow world of modern Evangelicalism, only to be abandoned by appetites that desire to hear something new and more novel;[103] or will it reveal itself as a continuing mechanism of doctrinal destruction for its hearers. In either case, the believer's responsibility is quite clear. The victory of our present contest is found in our righteous Advocate, the Lord Jesus Christ. His revelation of the Father is sufficient, both in his incarnation, and through His infallible, unified, and God-breathed message as delivered through His ordained Apostles and Prophets.

As the children of God, may we embrace no other message or authority, for apart from God's Word *alone* we have no other hope or surety in this life.

Soli Deo Gloria.

---

[103] Acts 17:21 (Now all the Athenians and the strangers visiting there used to spend their time in nothing other than telling or hearing something new.).

Appendix:

Another Conversation Parts 1-5

When the manuscript for this work was originally written, I immediately sent a copy of it to Bishop Wright himself in order to give him the opportunity to produce a critique of my work. Our exchange was brief, and yet I have found his comments to be quite telling. Thus, as a final wrap-up to *Indeed, Has Paul Really Said?* I will supply, within this appendix, a response to his criticisms and comments.

Appendix, Part 1

In his response, Mr. Wright delivered five points of analysis which will constitute the layout of this section. Thus, the following is a brief summary of what he supplied (as he said) "as a matter of urgency."[104] We will begin with Mr. Wright's disagreement over my use of the theological label *New Perspective* – especially since I associated it with his and E.P. Sanders' teaching. In his note to me, Wright pointed out that there are enormous differences in exegesis and theology between the proponents of the new perspective. As well, he took issue with my having associated him with E.P. Sanders, arguing that for the past twenty years he has written critically of Sanders' theology and exegesis of Paul, though admitting, parenthetically, that he has agreed with Sanders on some other matters. [105]

---

[104] Bishop Tom Wright, December 2nd 2007 Correspondence RE: "What Saint Paul Really Said..."
[105] Ibid.

Appendix

It is important that we begin with this point [though it was the third in his letter] since it unveils an interesting pattern in the Bishop of Durham's writings. As an observation, *I find that he seems frequently insistent that he is a unique arbiter of the NPP tradition, and this seems to be more prominent in his recent writings.* His dissatisfaction with my brief bio on him even reinforces this, such that my brief mention of the New Perspective along with Sanders' name, made matters uncomfortable for him. But the reader should note that my introduction of Wright was dramatically (even intentionally) brief:

> *"Most people reading this book will already be familiar with the teachings and background of Mr. Wright. Wright holds doctorate degrees from Merton College, Oxford University, along with several other honorary doctorate degrees from other institutions. Since 2003 he has served as the Bishop of Durham for the Church of England and has become very popular here in America, mostly due to his published books and other literature. Perhaps he is best known for his part in advancing the theological movement known as The New Perspective on Paul, in keeping with men like E.P. Sanders and James Dunn. The most significant impact of The New Perspective on Paul has to do with its transformation of the doctrine of justification and imputation."*

I crafted this bio with great care and brevity. I say brevity because I wanted to focus on Wright's teaching, rather than on his personal life and background. What I wanted to avoid was the problem of having to answer for the teachings of more than one man, knowing that addressing Wright's teaching would be a large enough task all by itself. Books that deal with multiple theologians, including exhaustive inquests into the background and personalities of such theologians, often become entangled in a cobweb of subjective argumentation, thus distracting the reader from the subjects of exegesis and theology. I had no interest engaging in such a venture at all. Ultimately, I only mentioned Sanders because Wright himself mentions him several times in his own work in question, the most prominent of which occurs on page 18:

> "It is a measure of Sanders' achievement that Pauline scholars around the world now refer casually to 'the Sanders revolution'. Even those who are hostile to his theories cannot deny that there has indeed been a great turn-around in scholarship, so much so that many books written before Sanders, or from a pre-Sanders standpoint, now look extremely dated and actually feel very boring – something no writer on Paul ought to be! Though I myself disagree strongly with Sanders on some points, and want to go a good deal further than him on some others, there is no denying that he has towered over the last quarter of the century much as Schweitzer and Bultmann did over the first half."[106]

Sanders' "towering" contribution to the subject of Pauline theology is upheld by Wright as "revolutionary," bringing about a "great turn-around in scholarship," though he qualifies this assessment with his strong disagreements on certain issues. Ultimately, Wright, by his own admission, is *advancing, or furthering*, key aspects of Sanders' own teaching. This is why I carefully used the word *advancing* with its central denotation. When one *advances* a movement or ideology they are, by definition, taking it further from where it stands. This, in conjunction with mentioning Sanders as a member of the NPP movement, comports with Wright's own words. While I can acknowledge that there are differences between Wright,

---

[106] Wright, Saint Paul, p. 18.

Appendix

Sanders, and Dunn (as there are always differences among any number of theologians, liberal or otherwise), their point of commonality should be clear: *all these men are presenting a new theology of Paul through the infusion of extrabiblical writings.* It is this theology of Pauline-*eisegesis*[107] that establishes a common thread between all three men in the broadest sense. This is true whether you refer to this movement as a *new perspective* or as a *fresh perspective:*

> "This will clear the way for a fresh presentation, in the following chapter, of what I have called a 'fresh perspective' on Paul (as opposed to the merely 'new' perspective, which is now somewhat less new than it was)..."[108]

I must leave it to Wright and Sanders to debate, among themselves, the differences between the words "new" and "fresh." Whatever nuanced word one wishes to use regarding such Pauline-redaction, the observant reader will probably understand that what these men are teaching is a clear innovation and departure from historic exegesis.

The danger that all these men present is this idea which assumes that the interpreter has the license to import extra-biblical influences (Jewish oral traditions, intertestamental writings [the Apocrypha & Pseudepigrapha], contradictory & extra-biblical history) into the mind and mouth of Paul. I addressed this error more thoroughly in *Chapter 3: The Righteousness of God & Paul's Apostleship.* But in summary, let me say that anyone who advocates such an *eisegetical* approach

---

[107] Eisegesis: the process of interpreting Scripture via the imposition of various extra-biblical ideologies.

[108] N. T. Wright, Paul, In Fresh Perspective, (Fortress Press, Minneapolis), p.40.

can effectively render any interpretive conclusion that they may desire, especially since the ideological realm of "second temple Judaism" is so vast, and not at all monolithic. Wright played this dangerous game in *What Saint Paul Really Said*, by suggesting that Paul was bound to the influences of Shammaite theology. By this infusion, he argued that Paul's notion of justification was eschatological, and had nothing to do with a forensic concept of immediate salvation through the imputed righteousness of Christ. Such a methodology as this permits the interpreter to turn on the spigot of extra-biblical influence when it suits his view of what Paul may have thought and meant in his writings. In like manner, the interpreter can turn the same spigot off when the extra-biblical influences prove to be inconvenient for his broader argument. The fact that any of these men should believe that Paul (an Apostle of Jesus Christ) would be committed to anything else but God's word is a dark presumption to begin with. I certainly grant that Wright, Sanders, and Dunn have their own conclusions about *what Paul really said* – but the common denominator between them all is this: *they are not exegeting Paul at all.*

Finally, I have noticed a pattern in Mr. Wright's writing which presents him as a bit of a theological soloist. In *What Saint Paul Really Said* he complains about the misunderstanding of Reformed and Roman Catholic theologians throughout the centuries, arguing that what divides Rome from Protestantism is nothing more than "petty" and "culture-bound" differences.[109] The sweeping nature of such a comment is breathtaking. With a world of Reformed and Catholic theologians sidelined as irrelevant, Wright appears as a bit of a maverick, because what

---

[109] Wright, Saint Paul, p. 158.

Appendix

he presumes to understand is that which no one else has comprehended for centuries. Additionally, he is often found judging his opponents as being guilty of all sorts of mischief; as those who mistreat the Apostle Paul in every conceivable way, whereby they "abuse him, misunderstand him, impose their own categories on him, come to him with the wrong questions and wonder why he doesn't give a clear answer, and shamelessly borrow material from him to fit into other schemes of which he would not have approved."[110] In this way Wright frequently stages his analysis of Scripture against a very grave backdrop, suggesting that most exegetes "routinely" marginalize certain passages as "throwaway" lines for a broader, systematic theology.[111] Language such as this leaves the reader waiting for someone to rescue them from the despair of corrupt exegetes, which then sets the stage for Wright to appear with the lifeline of his new (fresh?) perspective on Paul. I only mention this because of its repetition. For myself, it becomes distracting when reading him. Obviously, people write books because they believe that they are providing something that is helpful to others. But the best of authors do so with the aid of other brethren; never as an absolute soloist. For Mr. Wright, he may have declared himself to be independent from the NPP movement, having re-emerged as the leader of FPP. For myself, whether one calls it NPP or FPP, I must still call it as I see it. It is all an aberration from biblical exegesis; it amounts to a stilted understanding of Paul and his teaching; it results in a renunciation of justification by faith and it leaves the Bible in

---

[110] Ibid, p. 11.

[111] "Of course, this passage (Romans 1:3-4) has routinely been marginalized, and treated as though it were a mere throwaway introductory line, designed to curry favour with Jewish Christians in Rome..." Wright, Paul, In Fresh Perspective, p.44.

the dangerous position of being subject to the whim and will of every human interpreter imaginable.

In the end, there is nothing *new* or *fresh* about any of it.

Appendix, Part 2

Wright's attempt to distinguish his theology by calling it a "fresh" rather than a "new" perspective on Paul should not be surprising. By such a strained nuance as this, one should remember that this is actually quite typical of all theological innovationists – they have a need to be doctrinally flexible in their pursuit of that which is, to them, *new and appealing* – if even *fresh* and appealing. The desire for innovation and novelty is very much a part of our nature as fallen men such that, like the multitudes in Paul's time, many today like to spend their time "telling or hearing something new."[112] Ancient truth does not appeal to the natural man, but innovation, novelty, and sensationalism does. I begin with this point, as a transition from Part I to Part II of the appendix, in order to present Wright's next criticism. In his second point he took issue with the fact that I had chosen to critique his book *What St Paul Really Said*, noting that this work was "nearly ten years out of date." He went on to mention other works of his that he considered to be his more important and thorough treatments of the subject of justification: his "big" commentary on Romans in the New

---

[112] Acts 17:21: 21 Now all the Athenians and the strangers visiting there used to spend their time in nothing other than telling or hearing something new.

Appendix

Interpreters Bible (volume 10), and *Paul in Fresh Perspective*. Concerning this latter work, Wright highlighted the sixth chapter as providing a much more recent update on his views. Along with this he mentioned that he had heard, through friends, of one seminary professor who read his commentary on Romans and spoke approvingly of it. This seemed like an odd bit of evidence, especially since Wright later admitted that he had never confirmed the veracity of the matter. Finally, though Mr. Wright complained about the fact that *What St Paul Really Said* is over a decade old, he also stated, without equivocation, that he still stands by what he said in that work. [113] I was thankful for his input concerning his later works, and thus I accepted his offer to examine them as he prescribed. When I reviewed these works of his, my resolve to proceed with this book only increased. Concerning Mr. Wright's logic regarding the relevancy of his older works, I must say that in a weaker moment I might be tempted to accept such reasoning; however I must ultimately leave it to Mr. Wright to reconcile the following proposition regarding his book, *What St. Paul Really Said [WSPRS]*:

A. "[regarding WSPRS]...you are nearly ten years out of date."

B. "...I stand by what I said [regarding WSPRS]."

If Mr. Wright really stands by what he wrote over a decade ago, then no one will be "out of date" concerning his views. Concerning such logic, *Wright can't have it both ways.* This is the inherent problem that comes with any dynamic system of liberal theology. Such flexibility affords theologians the

---

[113] Bishop Tom Wright, December 2nd 2007 correspondence, RE: "What Saint Paul Really Said..."

Indeed, Has Paul Really Said?

opportunity to shift and change according to the need of the moment. This is why I have likened Wright's interpretive method to that of a secret decoder ring, one that can be adjusted as needed. Mr. Wright's infusions of extra-biblical influences, into the mind of Paul, enable him to create alternate and changing biblical codes in keeping with the latest adjustments in liberal thinking. His first decoder ring, as developed in *What Saint Paul Really Said*, was more limited in its application. This is apparent when one considers that Wright focused mostly on the range of views within Shammaite Pharisaism when redacting the Apostle Paul; however, in his subsequent writings (including his commentary on Romans) Wright expands his exegetical decoder ring by employing a broader range of ideas as presented in the intertestamental writings of the Pseudepigrapha. Thus, we can agree that he did offer some additions to that which he previously argued, but nothing in his subsequent writings actually refutes his past arguments, which is consistent with his own claim. All that Wright has changed is this matter of *theological variability and flexibility.* Having afforded himself the freedom to redact the Apostle Paul, by means of the broad corpus of Pseudepigraphal writings, N.T. Wright has increased the breadth of his interpretive license when expounding on the words of the Apostle Paul. This now leaves his critics with a more difficult task of pinning down the fallacious infusions found within his arguments:

> *"...it is of course important that we also contextualize Paul in his own day by noticing these same themes in second-Temple literature. There is no space to expound this in detail. I merely note that in very different writings, such as the Wisdom of Solomon, the Qumran literature and the apocalyptic writings such as 4 Ezra and 2 Baruch,*

Appendix

we find exactly these themes, albeit deployed in very different ways...Though Paul appears over the heads of the later texts to the Bible itself, his own reuse of the biblical themes possesses an easily recognizable family likeness to the other reuses of his day."[114]

We can credit Mr. Wright for his honesty regarding his intention to "contextualize" the Apostle Paul within the "themes of second-Temple literature." It is interesting that Wright affords himself such a license to infuse Pauline theology with the themes in second-Temple literature – and yet, as he says, "There is no space to expound this in detail." I can assure the reader that his brief book, *Paul, A Fresh Perspective*, at only 195 pages, could have handled at least some *"expounding"* on this issue. Those who present their arguments as being true, without performing the work of defending their positions, should "kindly withdraw from the lists."[115] For Wright, the inconvenience of presenting detailed arguments is easily handled by men like E.P. Sanders – the man with whom I so casually associated the Bishop of Durham:

"At this point at least I am fully on the side of E.P. Sanders when he argues that the covenant is the hidden presupposition of Jewish literature even when the word hardly occurs."[116]

The reason why Wright doesn't expand on some of his presuppositions is because men, like Sanders, have already done so in their own writings. In his book, *Common Judaism – Explorations in Second-Temple Judaism*, Sanders develops a system of thought concerning how the Jews viewed God's

---

[114] Wright, Paul, A Fresh Perspective, p. 25.
[115] Luther, The Bondage of the Will, p. 74.
[116] Ibid., p. 26.

covenant with the nation in terms of the intertestamental Jewish writings (i.e. Second-Temple Judaism). Thus, standing on the "towering" efforts of Sanders, Wright regards much of the Second-Temple Judaism argument as being unquestionably true; and it seems evident that he expects his readers to accept this paradigm of thinking as a conclusive fact, without having to do the work of justifying such a presumption.

For Mr. Wright, the presumption of a Sanders-Second-Temple-Judaistic influence on the New Testament writers constitutes an end of argument – having no need or room to expound the matter in a 195 page book. But this form of thinking isn't so easily reconciled with the Paul of Scripture who, soon after his conversion, was "confounding the Jews" "by proving that...Jesus is the Christ[117]...explaining and giving evidence" by *reasoning from the Scriptures.*[118] Paul did more than merely appeal "over the heads of the later texts" (intertestamental writings) – he ignored them entirely and appealed to nothing else but *Scripture alone.*

In the next section of the appendix we will further evaluate this proposition which says that there is a "family likeness" between Paul's writings and that of the Pseudepigrapha. To say that there is a likeness between Holy Writ and the doctrinal drivel found in books like *2 Baruch* is at best vague, and at worst, utterly deceptive. Concerning this final point, we will briefly look at the potential danger that can come to any expositor who chooses to herald such forms of thinking.

---

[117] Acts 9:17-23.
[118] Italics mine, Acts 17:1-3.

Appendix

Appendix, Part 3

When I first wrote the main body of this book, I intentionally erred on the side of a bare-bones exegesis, only occasionally citing theologians from church history. While this isn't my normal approach to any theological study, I certainly wanted to avoid the trap of being accused of merely repeating a certain *theological tradition* – an accusation that I knew Wright would be inclined to make. Yet despite my strenuous efforts to avoid stepping on any church-history cracks, Wright, unbelievably, delivered it anyway. In this next criticism of his, Wright began by insisting that he yielded to none in his working principle of Sola Scriptura. He then invited me to show him his error *exegetically*, in which case he vowed to follow my teaching "every inch of the way," surmising that if my complaint with him was based upon his differences with 16th century Reformers, as if to say that he is wrong, arrogant, dangerous, denying the gospel etc., then he would prefer scripture to tradition - even "the venerable tradition in which we ourselves have been nurtured."[119]

When I read this portion of his critique, I was amazed by the implied charge. In my book, my brief reference to the subject of church history dealt with Luther and his contest with Erasmus, but I did this only to reveal the fragility of modern debate. When one reads the scholarly and heated exchanges of

---

[119] Bishop Tom Wright, December 2nd 2007 correspondence, RE: "What Saint Paul Really Said..."

yesteryear, it becomes apparent that the sensitivities of the modern mind are a bit *too sensitive*. Being most concerned about the tone of my writings, I consulted Luther's rebuke of Erasmus in order to calibrate the reader's thinking about my own approach. Beyond this brief reference – I offered no specific systems of theology from church history. I would gladly have a debate over the exegetical issues relating to the doctrine of justification, provided that such exegesis is, in fact, derived from Scripture. Sadly, this isn't what Wright is doing at all despite his seemingly noble appeals. What Wright is actually doing is performing an exegesis of Jewish tradition blended with Scripture – the very concoction which Christ Himself opposed.[120] In the previous section of the appendix, I mentioned Wright's infusions of Jewish tradition by means of the intertestamental Jewish writings, the likes of which (we are told to believe) bear a "family likeness" to Paul's own mindset. Here again is the quote from Wright:

"...it is of course important that we also contextualize Paul in his own day by noticing these same themes in second-Temple literature. There is no space to expound this in detail. I merely note that in very different writings, such as the Wisdom of Solomon, the Qumran literature and the apocalyptic writings such as 4 Ezra and 2 Baruch, we find exactly these themes, albeit deployed in very different ways...Though Paul appeals over the heads of the later texts to the Bible itself, his own reuse of the biblical themes possesses an easily recognizable family likeness to the other reuses of his day."[121]

Wright didn't have the "space to expound" his point, and later refers to E.P. Sanders as his authority on the matter. Such a

---

[120] Mark 7:5-13.
[121] Wright, Paul, A Fresh Perspective, p. 25.

presumed QED is not *biblical* exegesis. In fact, if one were to impose the theology of, say, 2 Baruch to the Pauline corpus, you would end up with an entirely redacted Apostle. Consider the case of Manasseh. In 2 Chronicles 33, Manasseh's wickedness is clearly laid out before the reader. His debauchery and idolatry is breathtaking, but then something amazing took place:

> *2 Chronicles 33:12-13: 12 When he was in distress, he entreated the Lord his God and humbled himself greatly before the God of his fathers. 13 When he prayed to Him, He was moved by his entreaty and heard his supplication, and brought him again to Jerusalem to his kingdom. Then Manasseh knew that the Lord was God.*

Should there be any doubt concerning what took place within the heart of this wicked man, then consider the Lord's comparison of Manasseh to that of his son, Amon:

> *2 Chronicles 33:23: 23 Moreover, he [Amon] did not humble himself before the Lord as his father Manasseh had done, but Amon multiplied guilt.*

The beauty of Manasseh's life is that it tells the story of God's delight in the sinner who repents of his sin.[122] It was the same story that Paul told about himself:

> 1 Timothy 1:15-16: 15 It is a trustworthy statement, deserving full acceptance, that Christ Jesus came into the world to save sinners, among whom I am foremost of all. 16 Yet for this reason I found mercy, so that in me as the foremost, Jesus Christ might demonstrate His perfect patience as an example for those who would believe in Him for eternal life.

---

[122] Ezekiel 18:23: 23 "Do I have any pleasure in the death of the wicked," declares the Lord God, "rather than that he should turn from his ways and live?

But if we were to close our eyes and blindly embrace the presumed QEDs of N.T. Wright, we would expect to find the same theological "family likeness" of the Apostles within the intertestamental writings; but such is not the case. What we actually find is a mishmash of O.T. history, conjoined with some Jewish mythology and pharisaical traditions – including traditions like that of the Shammaite Pharisees who believed that entrance into heaven was achieved by means of a perfect righteousness as derived by a life of absolute obedience.[123] Remember that it was that middle group of those "in between" the thoroughly righteous and thoroughly wicked that later became the foundation of the extra-biblical teaching of purgatory. Thus, we must ask the question: what family likeness should we expect to find within the intertestamental writings? Will we find reflections of the Apostle Paul, or of the oral traditions of the Jews? Consider the following excerpt from the book of 2 Baruch as it tells the story of Manasseh:

2 Baruch 64:5-10 "But also against the two tribes and a half went forth a decree that they should also be led away captive, as thou hast now seen. ⁶ And to such a degree did the impiety of Manasseh increase, that it removed the praise of the Most High from the sanctuary. ⁷ On this account Manasseh was at that time named "the impious", and finally his abode was in the fire. ⁸ For though his prayer

---

[123] "'The School of Shammai declared, There will be three groups on the Day of Judgment: one of thoroughly righteous people, one of thoroughly wicked people and one of people in between. The first group will be immediately inscribed for everlasting life; the second group will be doomed in Gehinnom [Hell], as it says, 'And many of them that sleep in the dust of the earth shall awake, some to everlasting life and some to reproaches and everlasting abhorrence' [Daniel 12:2], *the third will go down to Gehinnom and squeal and rise again*, as it says, "And I will bring the third part through the fire, and will refine them as silver is refined, and will try them as gold is tried. They shall call on My name and I will answer them." Cohen, Everyman's Talmud, pp. 377-78 [See also the Babylonian Talmud, tractate Rosh Hashanah 16b-17a].

Appendix

was heard with the Most High, finally, when he was cast into the brazen horse and the brazen horse was melted, it served as a sign unto him for the hour. ⁹ For he had not lived perfectly, for he was not worthy—but that thenceforward he might know by whom finally he should be tormented. ¹⁰ For he who is able to benefit is also able to torment."[124]

For the Shammaite Pharisees, the idea of a "thoroughly wicked" Manasseh praying a prayer and being redeemed by God's grace in the eleventh hour of his life was probably too much for them to take. It didn't fit very nicely within the works-righteousness framework of their oral traditions. I find it amazing that the book of 2 Baruch makes reference to Manasseh's prayer, and yet he is said to be guilty of not having "lived perfectly" and is therefore given over to a fiery death as a sign of his eternal torment in hell. Or as William John Deane said in his book – *Pseudepigrapha: An Account of certain Apocryphal Sacred Writings of the Jews and Early Christians:*

"Baruch testifies that though his prayer was heard, he himself was lost. 'When he was placed in the brazen horse,' probably an image connected with the worship of Moloch, 'the figure was melted with the ardent heat, and he perished therein, a sign of the end that awaited him. For he had not lived a perfect life, nor was he worthy; but by this sign he learned by whom he was to be tormented hereafter.'"[125]

What Scriptural "family likeness" do we see in such a passage as 2 Baruch 64:5-10? It is not the family likeness of the Spirit of

---

[124] Pseudepigrapha of the Old Testament, ed. Robert Henry Charles (Bellingham, WA: Logos Research Systems, Inc., 2004), 2:515.

[125] William J. Deane, Pseudepigrapha: An Account of Certain Apocryphal Sacred Writings of the Jews and Early Christians, (T&T Clark, Edinburgh), p. 147.

Indeed, Has Paul Really Said?

God who carried along men to write, not the words and traditions of men, but the word of God. If there is a family likeness at all, it is the reprehensible likeness of the Shammaite Pharisees whose doctrines obviously stood in opposition to the message of grace in the eternal Gospel of God. One can't help but to wonder why anyone would imagine an Apostle of Christ writing to the churches under the theological and lexical influence of writings such as 2 Baruch. As noted before, the variability of these intertestamental writings leaves the liberal exegete with a great number of interpretive options. He can simply turn on, or off, the spigot of such writings according to his own needs and preferences; thus incorporating those texts that suit his arguments, while ignoring those that don't. But let the reader note the following: this is very similar to what the writer of 2 Baruch did. In order to preserve a system of works-righteousness, he had to modify the story of Manasseh by *turning off the spigot of 2 Chronicles 33 (verses 12-13, 23)*. In either case, we are not at all talking about biblical exegesis.

Any exegete who is being truly biblical will stand on the authority of God's word alone. Mr. Wright can claim that he yields to no one on the working principle of Sola Scriptura, but his exegetical actions belie his words. Rather than conducting biblical exegesis, Mr. Wright is popularizing what should be called extrabiblical exegesis – *which is exactly what it is.*

Appendix

Appendix, Part 4

The order of Wright's protests have been rearranged in this appendix in order to reveal the broader tapestry and connectedness of his comments. When considering the big picture of it all, a portrait begins to emerge: one which conjoins the scientific concepts of *accuracy* and *precision*. When observing Mr. Wright's repeated attempts to hit the bull's-eye of truth, it should be evident that he is both *inaccurate, yet precise (consistently off-target)*. Within the realm of science, the concept of scientific precision is an important and useful one, but in biblical theology *precision* holds no virtue at all. If we miss the mark of truth at all, we are never improved by being consistently wrong. Wright's *precise* errors are attributable to his consistent deference to the notion of second temple Judaism. It is for this reason that his pontifications about Pauline theology regularly miss the mark and stray into the dangerous territory of innovation: a domain that is very appealing to this postmodern generation of ours. Especially here in America, there is a rising theological trend which favors subjectivity and innovation, and it is for this reason that there has been a developing *symbiotic relationship* between men like Wright, and movements like the Emergent Church (EC).[126] I use the term *symbiotic* in order to acknowledge that, while there can be a degree of mutual *dependence* between two entities, this does not connote mutual *equality*. Such is the case with Wright and what is loosely

---

[126] Also referred to as the "Emergent Conversation."

termed as the Emergent Conversation here in America. Though there are distinctions to be found between Wright and the EC, one finds a brilliant convergence of theological innovation between the two. Wright's own innovations of Pauline doctrine have proven to be very appealing to the EC community, and even Wikipedia has noted such a connection:

> "Wright has been warmly received particularly by those who identify with the postmodern Emerging Church movement. He has welcomed the hearing he has gained from the Emerging Church, but noted his own commitment to historical, orthodox, and biblical foundations not always shared by the Emerging Church."[127]

For myself, I had noticed a kind of *family likeness* between some of the more prominent writers in the EC, and that of N.T. Wright; noticing too that some of these writers readily cited Wright as a kindred theologian. Because of my own concern over the EC here in America, I originally had included a few paragraphs noting that a kind of theological symbiosis existed between Wright and the EC. After mentioning Paul's rebuke of the Corinthian church for their complicity with error (2 Corinthians 11:1-4), I noted the following:

> For the church to engage in *friendly conversations* with errorists is plainly dangerous; and those who observe the complicity of leaders who do so will be inclined to entertain dangerous doctrines themselves. But in all of this we should remember that there is a need to be balanced in our application of the Apostle's warnings. While the church must certainly guard against mindless dialogue, she must also be careful not to hide from the very real problems which exist within the world of popular theology. Like Paul himself,

---

[127] N.T. Wright (Emerging Church), Wikipedia – the Free Encyclopedia (June, 2010).

Appendix

we too should be willing *to confront and expose* those teachings which stand opposed to the core tenants of the Gospel. And when genuine Christians observe others drifting towards such *catastrophic conversations*, they should be filled with the same passionate jealously that filled the heart of Paul. For a Christian to feel any other way means that he is content to watch others be drawn into spiritual adultery. *May it never be.*

I fear that Eve's example of deception is not only fitting for that ancient church at Corinth, but that today, through theological movements like the *Emergent Conversation* along with the advocates of the *New Perspective on Paul*, contemporary Christianity has been drawn towards several forbidden fruits of false teaching. From the doctrine of hell, the law, Christ's resurrection, the atonement, and justification by faith, many today are *bearing well* teachings that have nothing to do with biblical exposition. It is within this broader scope of concern that I write this critique of N.T. Wright's book *What Saint Paul Really Said.* He and others in the modern day have generated a seismic shock wave within the contemporary church, and one can only wonder what effects this will have in the near future, as well as on future generations. It is for this reason that I have decided to direct my attention towards one of the gravest errors being perpetuated today that has to do with the nature and work of *God's justification of the sinner*. Therefore, in order to make this my focus, I have chosen to critique the teachings of N.T. Wright on this matter, knowing that he is perhaps the most outspoken and the most read on this subject.[128]

As the reader will note from these two paragraphs, my association of the *New Perspective on Paul (NPP)* with the *EC* is based upon a "broader scope of concern" – and there is a very good reason for this. Whenever mentioning NPP or EC, broad strokes of the theological brush are required since these

---

[128] Original manuscript: Indeed, Has Paul Really Said?

theological groups are not at all monolithic in their convictions. However, what I do emphasize is their convergent appetite for *theological innovation*. It is this idea of rethinking Christianity, generation after generation, which is so troubling. Yet it is this troubling appetite which seems to connect Wright with the EC. In 2007, around the time that Wright and I had our brief exchange, an interview was recorded between Wright and EC advocate – Rob Bell:

> Wright: "I see possibilities for a post-post-modern Christian faith, which will look quite different from the modernist forms, due to the liberal and conservative stand-off which we still suffer from. And which will look different also from to the postmodern form, which the emerging church has to live in because that's where we are at the moment. But there will be something out beyond that. You can't put postmodernity on a pedestal and say, 'There we are. We've got it. Because we aren't modern anymore, this is where we've got to stay forever and ever.' You can't live like that. We have to see ourselves as in transition to something different, to something bigger ..."[129]

It is this notion of a Christian faith that is "in transition to something different, to something bigger..." that seems to draw Wright and the *de facto* supporters of the EC together quite often. However Wright, upon seeing my *broad* association of the NPP and the EC responded with incredulity. He stated that he had no idea why I would associate him with the emerging church movement. He acknowledged that he had been a guest at a few EC conferences, but that he was not "officially associated" with the movement, and that he had his own questions and concerns about various issues related to the

---

[129] Emergent Village Weblog, N.T. Wright on the Post-Emerging Church, based upon the video interview in Soularize 2007.

Appendix

EC.[130] At the outset, I must say that Mr. Wright's protest is a straw-man. I never actually said that he was "officially associated" with the EC movement, but more importantly, I'm not sure how anyone could be "officially associated" with such a loosely identified group. Should you ever doubt the amorphous nature of anything labeled as *Emergent* or *Emerging*, then simply "Google it" and discover the cornucopia of confusion that is the EC.[131]

Wright's complaint about being associated with the EC is not terribly dissimilar to his complaint about being associated with E.P. Sanders. In both cases Wright reveals his preference to be much more independent. Clearly, the EC has revealed a long-standing devotion to all things N.T. Wright. As an example of this, consider the following excerpt from Jeremie Begbie at the 19th Annual Wheaton Theology Conference [Jesus, Paul and the People of God: A Theological Dialogue with N.T. Wright, April 2010]. Jeremie Begbie, who is professor of Theology at

---

[130] Bishop Tom Wright, December 2nd 2007 correspondence, RE: "What Saint Paul Really Said..."

[131] Not only are the words emerging and emergent considered crucially different, but there are now "threads" and "streams" within the movement that are now considered to be worthy of distinction. "Many of those within the emerging church movement who do not closely identify with "emergent village" tend to avoid that organization's interest in radical theological reformulation and focus more on new ways of "doing church" and expressing their spirituality. Mark Driscoll, a leader within the emerging church, now distances himself from the "emergent thread." Some observers consider the "emergent stream" to be one major part within the larger emerging church movement. This may be attributed to the stronger voice of the 'emergent' stream found in the US which contrasts the more subtle and diverse development of the movement in the UK, Australia and New Zealand over a longer period of time. As a result of the above factors, the use of correct vocabulary to describe a given participant in this movement can occasionally be awkward, confusing, or controversial. Key voices in the movement have been identified with Emergent Village, thus the rise of the nomenclature "emergent" to describe participants in the movement. Some people affiliated with the relational network called "Emergent Village" do not identify with the label "emergent". [Wikipedia, Emerging Church]

Duke Divinity School, made mention of the symbiotic relationship between the EC and Wright:

> "...the pressure to rethink the church is stronger than ever. In a context marked by declining denominational membership, and an increasing number who may be attracted to the person of Jesus, and a broadly based spirituality but who shrink at the thought of joining a local congregation, the shape of an effective engagement of the church with our culture becomes an acute issue. Not surprisingly, ecclesiology is very much on the agenda. In the last 20 years or so, especially in the UK and the US, some of this rethinking has taken the form of clusters of networks sometimes called - Emerging Church. Many here will have been involved in these networks, as I have. Eager to find some form of corporate Christian life that can engage effectively with late or postmodern society, especially the unchurched, this movement forms a crucible of questioning and experimentation. Pressing hard issues about mission which has been raised very widely in the church today; indeed, far beyond Europe and North America. Delve into the literature and blogs of this movement, and lo and behold, we find that one of the commonest names cited is that of N.T. Wright."[132]

This example reveals that Wright's desire to be dissociated with the EC is, at best, disingenuous. No one is arguing that he has absolute agreement with such a broad community as the EC – who could? But who could honestly argue that there is not a significant relationship between them at all? If he felt so strongly about being dissociated from the EC, then he had the opportunity to refute Begbie when he had the chance. Perhaps in his 7PM session at the Wheaton Theology Conference, he could have begun by addressing Begbie with: "I have no idea

---

[132] Jeremie Begbie, 19th Annual Wheaton Theology Conference [Jesus, Paul and the People of God: A Theological Dialogue with N.T. Wright, Saturday, April 17th 2010, 10:35AM].

why you associate me with the emerging movement/church." But with a room filled with emergent-Wright *devotees*, such a public protest would have been rather awkward.

Appendix, Part 5

Though this section is the last in the series, it is a response to Wright's *first* critique of my original manuscript. I have chosen to save this matter for the conclusion of the appendix in view of its more sensitive nature. I say "sensitive" because it is my conviction that much of modern Christendom has entered into the dangerous realm of hero-worship, especially when it comes to their favorite Christian personalities. This issue has become so endemic within the Christian culture that very few perceive its influence. Let me qualify this point before proceeding, and before the reader assumes too much by what is being said in this section: we can thank God for those humble servants whose writings and examples of life are worthy of our time and imitation, however, such servants must never become the objects of our adoration or devotion. Even the Apostle Paul had the restraint and wisdom to offer an equitable rebuke to a church that was being corrupted by a similar problem:

> 1 Corinthians 1:12-13: 12. Now I mean this, that each one of you is saying, "I am of Paul," and "I of Apollos," and "I of Cephas," and "I of Christ." 13. Has Christ been divided? Paul was not crucified for you, was he? Or were you baptized in the name of Paul?

Indeed, Has Paul Really Said?

We must note that Paul had the humility to include himself in this list of names. We can thank God for such humility! Paul didn't succumb to the temptation of ignoring those who were showing deference to him above others; instead he rebuked all those who had reduced their Christianity to a personal following which divided Christ and His body. It takes a mature man to refute a personal following, but this was the man who had become an *Apostle and bond-servant of Jesus Christ*. Men who, in the modern day, suffer from such a personal following would do well to imitate this humble leader of the 1st century church. As an introduction to this final section, I must first mention that the modern church has become similarly *Corinthianized*, and this is a problem that carries with it profound implications. Throughout my years in pastoral ministry I have found that when speaking to others about doctrine, it is not uncommon to find a peculiar sensitivity among those who are highly devoted to a particular Christian leader. The modern Christian culture, replete with its well advertised television, internet and radio markets, has created a potential minefield for the local church. Pastors discover this most when they present an interpretation of Scripture which conflicts with the interpretation of someone's favorite Christian personality. When such contradictions arise, destructive and unnecessary conflicts can ensue. The solution to this problem is not to over-react by ignoring the best of what these leaders have to offer, however, one should exercise wisdom and caution when harvesting the most profitable elements of their teaching and example, remembering that they are fallible men. Ultimately, the church must embrace that Berean nobility which sends us back, not to human wisdom, but to the authority of God in the Scriptures. What I mention in this section is not rendered as a wholesale attack; instead it is an

Appendix

appeal to the very wisdom and discernment to which we are all called as Christians. As well, those who are viewed as being popular leaders in our day must be careful to exercise great caution when responding to controversies like NPP, or other dangerous doctrines like Federal Vision,[133] knowing that their commentary has the potential of leading others into greater discernment, *or possibly greater error*. All of this I mention at the outset because of who it is that Wright mentioned in his correspondence with me - John Piper. Wright mentioned that he had responded to Dr. Piper's developing work: *The Future of Justification*. Wright's response to Piper was given, as he said, at great length such that the final version of Piper's book was "considerably modified" by what Wright said. Wright went on to say that there were still a good number of misunderstandings in Piper's book, but that in the end - "it's much better than it was!"[134] After these claims, Wright went on to mention another man whose views were transformed once Wright had the opportunity to sway him. Concerning Dr. Piper, only the Lord knows the full detail of Wright's claims. The initial and final state of Piper's manuscript, before and after Wright sought to improve it, cannot be known. However, Wright's mention of Piper led me to read *The Future of Justification*. On the whole, *The Future of Justification* does a fair job of analyzing the details of Wright's theology; however, I would contend that it fails to confront the implications of Wright's errors. Additionally, his

---

[133] The focus of our study centers on N.T. Wright's teaching on justification, and the surrounding layers of NPP theology overall. Federal Vision theology, as a separate discussion, also carries with it many unsettling teachings that undermine and distort the Gospel, not the least of which is the notion of *covenantal election and decretive election*. These troubling matters will not be addressed here any further, but are only mentioned as a matter of record.

[134] Bishop Tom Wright, December 2nd 2007 correspondence, RE: "What Saint Paul Really Said..."

book is prefaced with commendations regarding Wright's exemplary commitment to Scripture, the resurrection of Christ,[135] the Gospel, justification,[136] and rigorous scholarship.[137] Taking this list in reverse order, what I would affirm is that he (Wright) may be well studied in contemporary scholarship; however his secularized ideology has infected his devotion to everything else in the list. I have already addressed the question of Wright's *demonstrated view* of Scripture in chapter four of this book, and would only add that a man's professed devotion to anything is best evinced by his actions, rather than words, or as the Lord taught his disciples:

Matthew 7:20: "So then, you will know them by their fruits."

Our Lord did not teach that we can know others by their *words alone*, instead, we see them best by means of their actual actions. Thus, I can profess to love evangelizing the lost all day long, but if I never tell others about the Savior then such words are revealed as a putrefying vapor. I am often reminded by others that Mr. Wright has in fact written a large work on the resurrection (740 pages). Perhaps it is on this basis that Piper affirmed Wright's commitment to this key doctrine, I don't know. But even the most cogent defense of the resurrection can be quickly gutted by a denial of the *implications* of such doctrine, and it is not uncommon to find our aforementioned problem of personality-adoration at the heart of such a denial. As an illustration of this the reader should note that Mr. Wright has co-authored a book[138] with Marcus Borg, who serves as

---

[135] John Piper, The Future of Justification, (Crossway Books, Wheaton IL), p. 15.
[136] Ibid, p. 17.
[137] Ibid, p. 25.
[138] The Meaning of Jesus: Two Visions.

Appendix

Professor of Religion at Oregon State University. Professor Borg denies the bodily resurrection of Jesus Christ, and in an interview with *The Australian,* Wright opined the following about his friend:

"I have friends who I am quite sure are Christians who do not believe in the bodily resurrection," he [Wright] says carefully, citing another eminent scholar, American theologian Marcus Borg, co-author with Wright of The Meaning of Jesus: Two Visions. "But the view I take of them - and they know this - is that they are very, very muddled. They would probably return the compliment. Marcus Borg really does not believe Jesus Christ was bodily raised from the dead. But I know Marcus well: he loves Jesus and believes in him passionately. The philosophical and cultural world he has lived in has made it very, very difficult for him to believe in the bodily resurrection. I actually think that's a major problem and it affects most of whatever else he does, and I think that it means he has all sorts of flaws as a teacher, but I don't want to say he isn't a Christian." [The Australian - Feature, April 13th 2005]

Notice that Wright charges Borg, not with outright error, but with being *"very muddled"* in his views. Now, if the Scriptures were not clear on this issue (the resurrection), then we would certainly have many *muddled* arguments over the matter, but the doctrine of the resurrection is one of the clearest and most central doctrines of Scripture:

Luke 24:36-39: 36. While they were telling these things, He Himself stood in their midst and said to them, "Peace be to you." 37. But they were startled and frightened and thought that they were seeing a spirit. 38. And He said to them, "Why are you troubled, and why do doubts arise in your hearts? 39. "See My hands and My feet, that it is I Myself; touch Me and see, for a spirit does not have flesh and bones as you see that I have."

John 2:13-22: 13 And the Passover of the Jews was at hand, and Jesus went up to Jerusalem. 14 And He found in the temple those who were selling oxen and sheep and doves, and the moneychangers seated. 15 And He made a scourge of cords, and drove them all out of the temple, with the sheep and the oxen; and He poured out the coins of the moneychangers, and overturned their tables; 16 and to those who were selling the doves He said, "Take these things away; stop making My Father's house a house of merchandise." 17 His disciples remembered that it was written, "Zeal for Thy house will consume me." 18 The Jews therefore answered and said to Him, "What sign do You show to us, seeing that You do these things?" 19 Jesus answered and said to them, "Destroy this temple, and in three days I will raise it up." 20 The Jews therefore said, "It took forty-six years to build this temple, and will You raise it up in three days?" 21 But He was speaking of the temple of His body.

When it comes to establishing the reality of Christ's bodily resurrection, Luke 24 and John 2 (among other texts) are unavoidably clear. As in the case of John 2:21, John used the Greek word - *sōmatos* > *sōma* - "body," which clearly identifies the reality of a physical, *bodily* resurrection. Thus Christ's reference to "this temple" clearly meant His own body, such that what would be physically destroyed through death would also be physically raised again in resurrection life.[139] Not even a mountain of modern "scholarship" can hide the clarity of that statement! It seems difficult to believe that anyone would want to defend the profession of a man who denies what Jesus Himself said He would do by His own power and authority (John 10:17). The test of Christian discipleship is not

---

[139] *Matthew 28:5-6: "......the angel answered and said to the women, "Do not be afraid; for I know that you are looking for Jesus who has been crucified. 6 "He is not here, for He has risen, just as He said. Come, see the place where He was lying."*

Appendix

determined by what we subjectively feel, think, or believe about others, but by that which Christ taught by His own authority: "If you continue in My word, then you are truly disciples of Mine."[140] Sadly, Borg's habit of playing fast and loose with the words of Christ does not end with the resurrection:

"I have learned that the message of Jesus was not about requirements, was not about here is what you must do or believe in order to go to heaven. It was about entering into a relationship to God now in the present—I see in that—wisdom teacher and a social father. And for me as a Christian what Jesus was like as a figure of history is a powerful testimony to the reality of the sacred or the reality of God. Being a Christian doesn't mean that one has to believe that Jesus really walked on water, or really multiplied loaves, and so forth. And I think that a literalistic approach to scripture has in the minds of many Christians become a major obstacle. I think I would be willing to say that the teaching of Jesus makes profound religious sense to me, whether Jesus said it or not. I'll simply say that I think given my understanding of Christianity there's all the room in the world for disagreement about whether the resurrection of Jesus involved something happening to his corpse, things like that. I grew up in a tradition which stressed correct belief, and I now see it's not about correct belief it all. It's about, you know, being in relationship to that to which all this stuff points. I think the resurrection of Jesus really happened, but I have no idea if it involves anything happening to his corpse, and, therefore, I have no idea whether it involves an empty tomb, and for me, that doesn't matter because the central meaning of the Easter experience or the resurrection of Jesus is that His followers continue to experience Him as a living reality, a living presence after His death. So I would have no problem whatsoever with

---

[140] John 8:31

archaeologists finding the corpse of Jesus. For me that would not be a discrediting of the Christian faith or the Christian tradition."[141]

Despite Mr. Borg's irreverent musings about the resurrection, the Apostle Paul settled the matter, once and for all, when he said:

1 Corinthians 15:17 "...and if Christ has not been raised, your faith is worthless; you are still in your sins."

With all of this we are reminded that what is at stake is the Gospel itself, and when men obfuscate the Gospel we must be careful to expose such obfuscation and refute it. Mr. Piper is free to have whatever opinion of Mr. Wright that he desires, but I must contend that a man who is willing to sideline the bodily resurrection of Christ, as a non-essential, should not be so freely affirmed as a lover of the Gospel.[142] By the evaluation of Holy Writ, I am of the conviction that Wright's *indirect* affirmations of heresy, along with his outright denials of imputed righteousness, place him in the category of those who are content to love and preach *another Gospel:*

Galatians 1:6-10: 6. I am amazed that you are so quickly deserting Him who called you by the grace of Christ, for a different gospel; 7. which is really not another; only there are some who are disturbing you and want to distort the gospel of Christ. 8. But even if we, or an angel from heaven, should preach to you a gospel contrary to what we have preached to you, he is to be accursed! 9. As we have said before, so I say again now, if any man is preaching to you a gospel contrary to what you received, he is to be accursed! 10. For am I now

---

[141] Rethinking Jesus, PBS Interview (March 28th, 1997), http://www.pbs.org/newshour/bb/religion/jesus_3-28.html.

[142] Piper, The Future of Justification, p. 17.

Appendix

seeking the favor of men, or of God? Or am I striving to please men? If I were still trying to please men, I would not be a bond-servant of Christ.

Even Paul had to contend with this same issue of personality adoration amidst his defense of the Gospel, otherwise why would it be necessary for Paul to add: "...If I were still trying to please men, I would not be a bond-servant of Christ." For the defenders of the Gospel, no amount of popularity, scholarship, or personal friendship should ever stand in the way of our defense and proclamation of the Gospel. An uncompromising stand for the Gospel will always yield polarizing results, but we must leave such outcomes to the Lord Himself.[143] In view of this, I was surprised by Piper's comments regarding Wright, both in his book and in public:

> "My conviction concerning N.T. Wright is not that he is under the curse of Galatians 1:8-9, but that his portrayal of the gospel - and of the doctrine of justification in particular - is so disfigured that it becomes difficult to recognize as biblically faithful."[144]

> Interviewer: "Dr. Piper, in your defense of the Gospel against N.T. Wright - Have you found Federal Vision theology of Doug Wilson to be another Gospel?" Piper: "No! That's easy. Doug Wilson doesn't preach another Gospel. Okay? I don't think N.T. Wright preaches a false gospel either; I think N.T. Wright preaches a very confusing Gospel."[145]

---

[143] 2 Corinthians 2:14-17.

[144] Piper, The Future of Justification, p. 15.

[145] Resurgence National Conference (Text & Context), February 26, 2008, Q&A with Mark Driscoll, John Piper, and Matt Chandler.

For Mr. Wright, his friend Marcus Borg is merely *muddled* in his views. For Mr. Piper, Wright is not preaching *another gospel*, only a *disfigured and confused one*.[146] For myself, I find the assessments of these men to be quite incredible. The doctrines of the bodily resurrection of Christ, as well as imputation and justification by faith, are all essential elements of the Gospel, such that their obfuscation or elimination necessarily yields that which is *another Gospel*. While I do not, and cannot, know the thoughts, motives, or intentions of Mr Wright or Mr. Piper, I feel compelled to offer this heartfelt exhortation, even to those who closely follow their writings and teachings: the temptation for *anyone* to withhold a needful corrective can be quite strong, especially when dealing with men of significant popularity or scholastic acclaim - *but such a temptation is dangerous*. Such personal adoration strips Christians of that *Berean* nobility[147] required of all of the King's soldiers. Whenever we lose the priority of *Sola Scriptura* we tend to degrade into defensive attitudes on behalf of the doctrines and practices of popular men. This is a perilous pattern of behavior, and none of us are exempt from such potential pitfalls. By mentioning these things, the reader should know that I have not strayed from the central subject of this work. While the focus of this book is on Mr. Wright and his teachings, this related problem of personality-adoration is proving to be a growing danger within the church, especially when it allows dangerous doctrines through the front door - *or even the back door*. As a pastor I have seen such troubling

---

[146] One must wonder how a "confused" and "disfigured" gospel can be called anything but *another gospel*.

[147] Acts 17:11: Now these were more noble-minded than those in Thessalonica, for they received the word with great eagerness, examining the Scriptures daily to see whether these things were so.

Appendix

patterns for years, and it only appears to increase in the present day. In view of this, I must express great concern for those who may be tempted to follow and parrot similarly insipid responses to doctrinal error based upon their admiration of a man. As the followers of Christ, *He* must increase, but *we* must decrease.[148]

Of all of Wright's "urgent" responses to my book, this final one stands out as that which reveals the potential dangers of any form of teaching that has been christened as new, novel, and *perceptively* scholastic. In particular, the greatest threat to the church is not found with those who are obvious errorists; instead, it is found with those whose error is cleverly veiled. False teachers do not introduce themselves to the church as dangers to the church, instead, they creep in *unnoticed* by the unfortunate permission of those whose discernment wanes.[149] For this reason, Christ's shepherds must never let down their guard in view of the shine and sheen of modern "scholarship." When they do, they subject the sheep to all forms of doctrinal danger, and this is no small matter. My concern regarding Wright's teaching is not that the doctrine of justification merely fails to flourish therein, but that it is doubly dead and uprooted.[150] Ultimately, the point of exposing these matters is not that they would be known to no specific end, but that those who have erred, or perhaps misspoken, would reconsider these matters very carefully. In view of justification's centrality to the Gospel overall, any other consideration would be harmful; even dangerous.

Soli Deo Gloria.

---

[148] John 3:30.
[149] Jude 3-4.
[150] Jude 12.

Index

Index

2 Baruch, 124, 126, 128-132

4 Ezra, 124, 128

Abraham, 26, 34, 36-37, 82-84

Agrippa, King, 72, 73, 75, 77

Amon, 129

Atonement, 13, 84

Borg, Marcus, 143, 148

Christ: Advocate, 17, 61, 63, 64, 66, 93, 94, 95, 97, 114; Atonement, 96; Mediator, 94; Priesthood, 46, 47, 51, 52, 62, 97; Propitiation, 35, 93, 96, 97; Sacrificial Substitute, 57, 64, 66; The *Paraclete*, 97; The Righteous, 17, 93, 94, 95, 96, 97, 98; Victory, 92; Witness, 47

Church: Doctrinal Danger, 102, 149; False Teachers, 149; Persecution, 70, 76, 78

Circumcision, 37, 80-81

Contemporary: Compromise, 10
Covenant: New, 48, 50, 51, 52, 56, 90; Old, 45, 48, 50-52, 63

Deception: *anexesthe*, 12; Corinthian, 11

E. P. Sanders, 14, 21, 69, 116, 117-120, 125-126, 129, 137

Ecclesiology, 21, 62, 69, 138

Ecumenism: Catholic and Protestant, 22; Eucharist, 22; False, 10, 21, 22, 104-107

Eisegesis: *ad-hominem*, 58; Argument of Omission, 56, 57, 76; Extrabiblical Literature, 101, 119, 132; Q.E.D., 31, 129

Emergent Conversation, 13, 133-135

Erasmus, Desiderius, 15, 85, 127

Federal Vision, 141, 147

Gehinnom, 83-84, 105, 130

God: Condemnation, 33; Creation of Man, 111; Glory of..., 38, 107; Jealousy, 13; Jewish Courtroom, 42, 43, 44, 45, 46, 48, 51, 56, 57, 58, 66, 74, 103; Lovingkindness, 32, 34, 35; Our Righteousness, 88; Peace with..., 37, 62, 95; The Potter, 111-113

Gospel, *Another*, 146, 147

Hillel, 70, 82, 110, 113

Idolatry, 92, 107, 129

Judgment: Deuteronomic, 46, 49, 54; Eschatalogical, 37, 55, 83, 85; Witnesses, 46, 49, 50, 51, 54

Justification: By faith, 37; By Works, 82, 83, 84, 105, 130; Covenant Faithfulness, 20, 21, 26, 28, 30, 31, 36, 38, 39, 63, 66, 67; Ether, 58

Lexical Analysis: "Creative", 42; *"trick of throught"*, 48, 62, 63; *Forensic*, 34, 35; Oversimplified, 23, 30, 31, 36, 63, 120, 136

Luther, Martin, 15, 85, 128

Manasseh, 129, 130, 131, 132

Messiah, 28

Mishnah, 71, 77, 82

Monergism, 104

Paul: Apostle of Christ, 17, 55, 71, 79, 80, 81, 103, 111, 120, 132; Former Pharisee, 72; Not a Man-Pleaser, 147; Saul of Tarsus, 67, 69, 70; Zeal, 77

Pharisees: Gamaliel, 67, 69, 70, 75, 76, 77, 78, 79, 81, 103; Rabbinic Devotion, 76; Shammai, 67, 68, 69, 70, 71, 76, 78, 79, 80, 81,

82, 83, 84, 85, 86, 94, 105, 106, 107, 110, 111, 113, 120, 124, 130, 131, 132; Traditions, 84, 119, 130

Piper, John, 141, 142

Pseudepigrapha, 71, 119, 124, 131

Purgatory, 83, 106, 130

Reformation, 16, 99
Regeneration, 80, 81, 92

Resurrection, 13, 105, 106, 135, 142, 143, 144, 145

Righteousness:
Connotative sense, 23, 27; Denotative sense, 17, 23, 24, 25, 27, 29, 39, 66, 73, 88; Ethical, 24, 25, 26, 27, 88, 91, 92, 97; Forensic, 17, 25, 26, 27, 42, 43, 44, 45, 46, 55, 63, 66, 88, 91, 92, 93, 97, 120; Greek, 23; Hebrew, 23; Imputed, 22, 31, 38, 57, 58, 59, 120, 146; Infused, 22; Old English, 24; Theocratic, 25, 27, 88, 91, 92, 97

Sadducees, 73, 78

Sanhedrin, 73

Scripture: Authority, 106; Bereans, 140, 148; Inerrancy, 89; Sufficiency, 99; Unity, 90

Scriptures: Inspired, 95

Second-Temple Judaism, 125

Septuagint, 30, 39

Serpent, 11, 18, 102

Sin: Imputation, 60

Soteriology, 21, 62, 69, 94

Synergism, 104

Talmud, 82, 83, 84, 110, 130

Proverbs 3:5-18:

5 Trust in Jehovah with all thy heart, And lean not upon thine own understanding: 6 In all thy ways acknowledge him, And he will direct thy paths. 7 Be not wise in thine own eyes; Fear Jehovah, and depart from evil: 8 It will be health to thy navel, And marrow to thy bones. 9 Honor Jehovah with thy substance, And with the first-fruits of all thine increase: 10 So shall thy barns be filled with plenty, And thy vats shall overflow with new wine. 11 My son, despise not the chastening of Jehovah; Neither be weary of his reproof: 12 For whom Jehovah loveth he reproveth; Even as a father the son in whom he delighteth. 13 Happy is the man that findeth wisdom, And the man that getteth understanding. 14 For the gaining of it is better than the gaining of silver, And the profit thereof than fine gold. 15 She is more precious than rubies: And none of the things thou canst desire are to be compared unto her. 16 Length of days is in her right hand; In her left hand are riches and honor. 17 Her ways are ways of pleasantness, And all her paths are peace. 18 She is a tree of life to them that lay hold upon her: And happy is every one that retaineth her.

www.ingramcontent.com/pod-product-compliance
Lightning Source LLC
Chambersburg PA
CBHW020003050426
42450CB00005B/293